Praise for previous work

"It takes courage to offer a way forward, courage to name some of the failures of the past, courage to offer a diagnosis and prognosis that require actual change in lifestyle. That's what Jack Reese offers in these pages, and I pray many readers take this positive, honest, and challenging book to heart."

—BRIAN D. McLAREN
author of *Faith After Doubt*

"With impeccable scholarship and vivid storytelling, this book is a kind of wistful love song to a heritage that the author plainly loves and a call to a future fashioned by our better angels."

—RANDY HARRIS
founding director of the Contemplative Ministers' Initiative

"In this moving, personal account of his own tribe of Christians, Jack expresses the struggle of all Christians to tell the truth about themselves, to see the pain of others, and to both receive and extend God's outrageous, extravagant outpouring of grace."

—KENNETH R. GREENE
founding pastor of Metro Christ's Church, Cedar Hill, Texas

"With the skill of a master storyteller and the bluntness of an Old Testament prophet, Jack Reese walks hand in hand with members of his own church family back in time to the place where their story began in order to pick up resources absolutely necessary to continue their journey into the future."

—WES CRAWFORD
author of *Shattering the Illusion*

grace, sideways

field notes of a doubting believer

JACK R. REESE

WILLIAM B. EERDMANS PUBLISHING COMPANY
GRAND RAPIDS, MICHIGAN

Wm. B. Eerdmans Publishing Co.
2006 44th Street SE, Grand Rapids, MI 49508
www.eerdmans.com

Published 2026
Printed in the United States of America

32 31 30 29 28 27 26 1 2 3 4 5 6 7

ISBN 978-0-8028-8589-0

Library of Congress Cataloging-in-Publication Data

Names: Reese, Jack Roger author
Title: Grace, sideways : field notes of a doubting believer / Jack R. Reese.
Description: Grand Rapids, Michigan : William B. Eerdmans Publishing Company, [2026] | Summary: "A seasoned pastor shares insights gained over fifty years about how doubts can deepen faith and provide an opening to encounter God"—Provided by publisher.
Identifiers: LCCN 2025024638 | ISBN 9780802885890 paperback | ISBN 9781467470520 epub
Subjects: LCSH: Faith (Christianity) | Belief and doubt
Classification: LCC BV4637 .R43 2026 | DDC 234/.23—dc23/eng/20251119
LC record available at https://lccn.loc.gov/2025024638

For MaLesa—

who has walked beside me through the ache and the wonder
and showed me God when I could not see

CONTENTS

for

INTRODUCTION

Faith never rises from the soil whole. It pushes upward, seed to bud to fruit, through setbacks and seasons, in innocence when the questions are gentle and the answers safe, in the wonder of prayers fulfilled, in the uneasy waiting when hearts crave any answer at all, through confessions laid bare to the dark, in hope that lifts its face to the morning. Faith is a mongrel. It is mixed, blended, crossbred, full of counterforces and contrasts, seeking wholeness, seeking light.

Doubt is crucial to these intertanglings of faith. To say doubts are mixed with faith is like saying wet is mixed with rain. Doubt is an indispensable voice in our spiritual discernings. Sometimes it leads. Sometimes it sits quietly in the corner, waiting to be noticed. But it's always near, assuring us that the strength of our faith doesn't depend on having all the answers but on choosing to believe anyway.

There will be days when faith goes quiet, when trust seems voiceless or afraid. Wait. Lean in. Stillness is necessary for faith's ripening, which springs from both our devotion and our doubt. But doubt is not unbelief. Its presence does not mean faith is dead. Doubt, rather, nourishes faith, keeping it from decaying into arrogance. Or apathy. What blooms from that soil may be slower, may be smaller, than the pumped-up, hollowed-out faith that avoids asking the hard questions, but it's real. Not unbruised but real. And real faith will last.

My friends and I were sitting at a table, eating the little hamburgers that are popular in that city—more like dinner rolls stuffed with a small square of meat and topped with a pickle. Tiny but addictive. We were young—part grown-up, part child, one moment silly, the next moment earnest. We talked about baseball and school and church. And about our faith. It wasn't overly heavy or intense. Actually, it was quite sweet. But for me, that conversation more than five decades ago was a marker, a thread of questions, apprehensions, hopes, and yearnings that has interwoven every relationship, every event, every conflict, every triumph, every heartache and risk and promise of my life from my late teenage years all the way to the swift ride I took, strapped to a gurney in the back of an ambulance, unexpectedly, a little less than a month ago.

My hospital stay was not long, but it was intense. I'm home now, still mostly in bed. I hate that part. I tend to be an active sort of person, rarely sick, never in the hospital. So I'm antsy. But I can't really go much of anywhere until we figure out what's the matter with me—other than my regular and ordinary quirks, obsessions, and pathologies.

In a few days, I officially retire from the last full-time ministry of my life. Of course, I've said that before, but I really mean it this time. Unless God sends me something special—if God, in fact, does that sort of thing. Or is it my ego that seems to fall for the things that appear to be special? The whole will of God thing isn't always easy to sort out.

But at the moment, I find myself with an unusual amount of free time. I could lie here and watch the news all day. It's possible something interesting will happen in the world of politics. Then again, I don't think Lesa and I can afford the antianxiety medicines or the psychiatric care I would require if I did that for a week. Or the rest of the day. So instead, I think I might try to find some peace with the inner wrestlings of my heart, the kind that a lot of folks have if we're honest: What do I do with my doubts? It's a quandary, this tug-of-war between faith and doubt. Though, in all honesty, it feels more like tug than war. Might these two seeming antagonists be more friendly than we have imagined? I'd better connect my laptop to a charger. This might take some time.

~

I was loud that night as I ate those little burgers with friends. Louder than usual, in multiple ways. First of all, my clothes were loud. I understand this only in retrospect. At the time, they just seemed normal, if a little dressier than usual. My slacks were a pale peach, made of polyester of course, with a wide, dark blue leather belt cinched snugly just below my hips. The hems of each pant leg were shaped, cut, and sewn into a full bell bottom, hanging about a quarter of an inch above the sidewalk, almost completely covering my dress shoes, which were made of blue leather, freshly polished, over two-inch heels. I wore a sporty dress shirt with an extra-wide collar and big dark blue stripes. Sharp, I thought to myself when I looked in the mirror earlier that day. Who knew how quickly such handsome clothes would go out of style? A shame, really. At least the colors. Slacks made of polyester deserved a long and painful death.

It wasn't just my clothes. My voice was loud. I was telling stories, lobbing wisecracks at the pack of teenagers walking with me down the riverfront. The whole group was loud, all of us. We were laughing, joking, teasing, and oblivious to everyone and everything around us. These were kids from the youth group, and I was their leader, young and confident, with faith in God and in myself, though perhaps not in that order.

It's possible that hiring someone so inexperienced to shepherd forty or fifty kids for the summer was unwise, if not downright crazy. I was nineteen, about to begin my second year of college. For three months, parents at the church looked to me to guide their teenage kids. They assumed I knew what I was doing. The sad thing is, so did I.

I loved every minute of those summer months. It's the sort of work I had always dreamed of doing. Besides, we were in St. Louis, Missouri, one of the great cities of the world. I had come from a much smaller town in a very different part of the country. I was in awe. Eight or ten of us had gone out on the town. It was a Sunday evening after our worship service, a common ritual among many churches in those days, expected if not mandatory for church members. Not coming together for a service each Sunday evening would have been as appalling then as canceling Christmas today.

We walked past the Gateway Arch, the towering silver monument standing bow-legged and confident on the banks of the Mississippi River, celebrating St. Louis's role in the westward expansion of the United States. We were a couple of blocks from old Busch Stadium, where I got to watch some of the greatest players in the history of baseball, like Steve Carlton, before he broke our hearts and left for Philly. And Bob Gibson, the great righthander. Joe Torre was the Cards' catcher. Lou Brock set the major league record for stolen bases. All were All-Stars. All are in the Hall of Fame. Busch Stadium was pretty close to the center of the universe. This ministry thing was turning out pretty well.

We talked about the Cards and school and girlfriends and boyfriends and music and all the topics common to teenagers everywhere. We laughed and teased as we made our way past the Arch, blissfully unaware of the darker history of the area, tales that cast shadows over the storylines of our lives, had we been able to see.

The Old Courthouse was less than a two-minute walk away. In 1847, a federal court met there and denied Dred Scott, the longtime slave, his freedom. A decade later, after further trials and conflicting verdicts, the US Supreme Court ended the legal wrangling. They held that no person, not just Mr. Scott but no person, who was descended from Africans, whether slave or free, had any legal claim to either citizenship or freedom. The shocking decision, condemned by half the nation and lauded by the other half, pushed the country to the brink of war. This famous courthouse was just a few steps away, but we were unaware of the drama hidden behind its walls and unconcerned about the consequences this city still bore as we bantered our way through the park.

Just west of us was Pruitt-Igoe, a blocks-long complex of thirty-three high-rise projects housing mostly Black families that, for reasons too numerous to count and too tragic to describe in a short paragraph, had been allowed to deteriorate into monuments of civic ineptitude and human misery. The horrors were going on then. Right then. But we were white kids from the suburbs and had no idea how ignorant we were of what was happening in the city or what it had to do with anything that mattered to us.

And then, of course, there was the whole nineteenth-century westward expansion. Turns out there had been a lot of people already living out west. The newcomers, like my own ancestors, were the immigrants, the outsiders and occupiers of the land. Wherever we live, our history and the history of our people, like faith itself, is flecked with shadows.

But I wasn't interested that night in the difficult stories. I wasn't looking for shadows. This was an evening out with the kids in the youth group, and we were having a blast. We sat down at a place with outdoor tables and chairs, eating the tiny burgers and tasty fries and talking. A couple of older high school boys sat at my table. We talked about our lives and about the future. The conversation had become serious.

One of them said, "I don't always like church. Church isn't always easy for me."

"I get it," I told him. "It isn't always easy for me either."

"No, you and I aren't talking about the same thing," he said. "I'm not like you. I'm not a minister. I don't always know what I believe. Sometimes I have doubts."

I didn't hesitate. "Yeah, me too," I said.

Maybe I should have thought about it before I responded. Maybe I should have said, "Oh now, doubts are the distractions that the devil sends you. Just give it all to God. Try not to have negative thoughts. You can believe your way through all those doubts. Maybe I can help." But I didn't believe that. Still don't. What I said was simply, "Me too."

The table was silent for a minute. That can't be right, they started saying. You're a minister. Well, I argued, I'm not really a minister. I'm just a college kid. But I'm telling you, sometimes I have doubts.

It might have been the first time I had said such words out loud, but it wasn't the first time I had doubted. Not so much as a child. As with most young children, the truths seemed absolutely clear to me then. But as a teenager, I began to have questions. I was no longer sure that my church was right about everything. I began to suspect that no church was right about everything. The Bible itself, in fact, didn't seem to be clear about everything. Otherwise, there wouldn't be so many differences among Christians. Maybe this lack of clarity in Scripture was the point. Maybe that's the way God intended it. Maybe we don't know all the answers. Maybe the problem is our need to make everyone else agree with us.

The questions over those teenage years kept coming. Why did God seem to answer the prayers of some people but not others? Why did God appear to bless white people more than my Black friends? Why was one of my friends told he couldn't serve communion because his hair was too long? Why did God care about how long anyone's hair was or whether I supported or opposed the Vietnam War or whether a girl could offer a prayer at the dinner table or in the youth group or from the pulpit on Sunday morning?

I don't know exactly where those questions came from. Perhaps it was the environment I had been raised in, the freedom my brothers and I felt to talk about things with our parents and each other, the openness, at least in part, to disagree. Perhaps it was growing up in a college town where it's normal to suspend judgment, change your mind, or say "I don't know."

Whatever its origins, I told my friend the truth that night. I did, in fact, struggle with my faith, just as he did. Maybe I was being simplistic, but I told him I thought it was normal to have doubts. I thought that's what it meant to have faith. And so those were the sorts of things we talked about that unforgettable summer, in the shadow of Busch Stadium and the Old Courthouse near the Gateway

Arch, when I was a teenager, when the whole world was still in front of me.

Twelve summers later, I would be a young senior pastor of a large church in another city. Within a few years, I would serve as a professor and seminary dean. I would become a community activist in a blighted urban neighborhood not all that different from Pruitt-Igoe. I would have my spiritual life transformed by a Black church. I would retire in order to write, only to be asked to serve in full-time ministry again. But at no point through all those years and in all those life situations had I fully come to grips with my doubts and my faith.

I needed time. I needed to stop. I needed to turn the drivenness button off, if I could find it. Perhaps when I retired, again. Perhaps then I would have the time. Except for the garage that needed to be organized and the front lawn that was showing signs of despair and the tomatoes and herbs we wanted to plant out back and the trips we wanted to take and the grandkids we wanted to see. Oh, and the thriving new company Lesa and her business partner had just launched, which, I don't know, might need my input about something or other. But after those things were done, then I would have the time to think about my faith. Maybe then.

~

Our air conditioner was turned down low, chugging hard to overcome the heat and humidity. I was fighting sleep a little, partly because I was hot, partly because I was cold. I became aware of the numbness in my right arm only gradually. I wasn't fully awake when the numbness turned to tingling, starting at my fingertips and creeping up to my shoulder. I couldn't seem to rub it out. Lesa, who apparently has a sixth sense about such things, was up immediately, asking questions. Whatever this was now had my attention. Should I be worried? Am I having a stroke?

I waited about half a second to make sure that what I was about to say to her was factually correct because, if so, I knew there would be consequences. It was. There were. "The right side of my face is starting to feel numb," I told her. Her fingers were dialing 9-1-1 before I could finish the sentence. The emergency team—it seems like there were about sixteen of them, but I'm sure that's not right—was coming through the front door in less than five minutes, checking my blood pressure, setting up various machines, and placing little suction cups under my shirt that I knew, when removed, would pull half the hairs off my chest. Which is to say about three.

Having a bedroom full of EMS workers probing me was sobering. I didn't think I was going to die, though I didn't know for sure. I had the sort of out-of-body sensation I've sometimes read about—a sense that I was observing all the action from above rather than from within, watching myself try to answer questions from the paramedics, at one point markedly slurring my words. Yes, this was serious, the sort of scene when serious Christians ask serious questions about their faith.

When it's just the everyday stuff, we don't typically worry a lot about faith and doubt or ponder the inevitability of our own death. We live, work, play, eat, sleep, cry, laugh, argue, worry about our weight, fuss at bad drivers, thumb our smartphones, binge on Netflix, and participate in the ordinary endeavors of life. At least most of the time we can do so without experiencing a crisis of faith or speculating about whether God is directly involved in our day-to-day activities or whether God cares about what happens to us. There are times, however, when one's faith in God is more than a minor curiosity. Turns out being strapped into an ambulance on the way to the hospital in the middle of the night is one of those times for me.

I live with doubts. Lots of them. There are many things I'm simply not sure of. It's not that I live my life questioning God about everything. I don't see suffering on the news and ask how a loving and all-powerful God could allow such a thing. At least not every time. I'm not always wondering if there's anyone out there hearing my prayers. I'm not paralyzed by my doubts. But they are close by.

I recognize the whole conversation about doubt can be unnerving to some. A lot of Christians believe that doubts are bad, even sinful, that doubting is the same as not believing, that to entertain doubt is to sabotage one's own faith, and why would anyone do that? Surely, it's better to avoid doubts entirely, in the same way a person would avoid drinking bleach with dessert or would stay away from bedbugs or the Ebola virus.

I do see the concern about doubt. I'm sympathetic. I'm just not convinced that attempting to reject the doubt in our lives is right or healthy. Doubts are built into the equation, so I think we need to face them head-on. Moreover, and this may be a harder point to swallow than your decision about bleach, I think doubts have benefits. They're important to a person's faith. If we have no doubts, our faith will likely end up anemic. Or dead. That's what I want to explore here, how doubts can deepen faith, how faith may provide an opening to encounter God, and how our faith will influence the way others see God.

~

It would help, I'm sure, if I explained what I mean by faith and doubt. Here's a first-blush run at it, though we will need to take time to let these ideas ripen a bit in the coming chapters.

Faith, at its heart, is a response to a couple of big questions. The first is, "Do I trust God?" Faith's answer is yes, even when you doubt. Sometimes you trust more, sometimes less. Sometimes your faith is teeming with life. At other times, you're hanging on by a hair. But on the trust question, faith leans in.

Asking the question about trust helps us focus on what's important about faith, on what faith is and what it is not. Faith is not primarily a mental acknowledgment of something. It's not just agreeing to certain facts or principles. We often talk about faith like that, about adhering to *the* faith. The faith, as a set of doctrines or denominational structures and commitments, is a perfectly legitimate use of the word. It's just not what we're talking about here or how the word is generally used in Scripture.

Faith—having faith, expressing faith, responding in faith, being faithful—is something else, something more. Faith is not a thing we gain or learn or acquire. We don't own faith as if it were a matter of intellect and will, the result of keen learning skills and good decision-making. If I have faith, as opposed to believing this or that doctrine, then I am engaged in something, connected to something, longing or aching for something.

The poet Christian Wiman describes the spiritual quest that many of us are on as "that burn of being that drives us out of ourselves, that insistent, persistent gravity of the ghost called God."[1] Somehow, Wiman's words resonate with my own experience with faith, though I couldn't possibly tell you exactly what it means or feels like. No word or string of words can fully describe such encounters with holiness, these occasions of deep, spiritual longing, which, for many of us, are like the vapor trails of faith. This sense of longing is part of faith's nature. It can provide the fuel, the urgency, for what faith is and does.

God is the primary actor in our faith. Faith is God's gift. We don't manufacture it. At the same time, our faith also acts—though, ironically, faith's actions are distinctly passive in nature. The active part of faith is not so much the doing of something as the hard work of letting. Faith, at its heart, is about relinquishing, about receiving. It is pulled more than it pushes. In that sense, the verb form of faith is not "to believe" but "to trust." Trust is about surrender. Healthy doubt nudges faith to let go.

When the question is about trust, the opposite of faith is not doubt but unbelief, and those are different things. Doubt is on faith's side. Doubt helps us figure out what's at stake. Doubt asks the important questions. Is there a God? Is God near? Is God for me? Does God care? Is God trustworthy? Or, more personally, should I trust God enough to let go of my will?

By asking these sorts of questions, doubt makes faith as hard as it should be. Easy faith tends to fail when things get tough, often because the tough questions were never asked. Repressing one's doubts often ends up opening the very door to unbelief we were trying to slam shut. A dose of healthy doubt, in contrast, provides a safety net for faith, keeping it from falling into unbelief. Faith's answer to the trust question is yes. Yes, I do. Yes, I will. Until that happens, nothing else about our spiritual journey will make much of a difference.

But there's a second crucial question that faith faces: "Do I know for sure?" That's a very different question than the one about trust. Faith's answer is an emphatic no. It has to be. I don't know for sure what God is up to. I don't understand all that faith is or all that faith does. I don't know all the answers. Faith, like God, is mysterious, and defining the mysterious with absolute confidence is absurd. And dangerous. I believe God is present with us and in us, but I can't say with total confidence that God did or did not do this or that. Things happen, but I don't always know why. Maybe God was involved but maybe not. On this question, the opposite of faith is not doubt but certainty.

Doubt keeps faith from falling into the trap of thinking it can grasp the divine mysteries. There are things we don't know. If faith knew, it wouldn't be faith. It would be sight, and our relationship with God is not based on sight. Faith says, "I don't know for sure, but I will trust anyway." Doubt's role is to keep a check on our own arrogance.

I hear the objections. Doesn't the Bible condemn doubting? After all, the Epistle of James says, "Ask in faith, never doubting, for the one who doubts is like a wave of the sea, driven and tossed by the wind."[2] I get it. In fact, I've used that objection myself. English, frankly, doesn't help us a lot here. We're all aware of words that can be used both positively and negatively. Like, is discrimination good or bad? Well, it depends. Are you talking about discriminating among ideas or discriminating against certain people? Or judging. Is it okay to judge others? The Bible clearly warns against judging. Plainly, "Do not judge."[3] But some sorts of judging are necessary. Simon answered a question from Jesus well, and Jesus told him, "You have judged rightly."[4] Meaning depends on context.

The root meaning of the word in James is to separate, distinguish, discern, judge, or discriminate. It can be a good thing, like the way the word is used in the Epistle to the Hebrews, "the mature . . . have been trained by practice to *distinguish* good from evil."[5] This same word is used in James but toward a different end. Though it's often translated as "doubt," the basic meaning is still the same—to distinguish or judge—but in this context it's an inner conflict, a paralysis that comes from second-guessing God or hesitating, like a kid standing at the edge of the pool too afraid to jump into her father's arms. In other words, it's a lack of trust, the very issue we're trying to get at here. Trust is the key. Faith is activated by trust like dough is activated by yeast.

Faith and doubt are not binary choices. It's not like we're deciding between this or that, black or white, in or out, yes or no, faith or doubt. It's not like a computer program based on a binary number system. The answer to a computer's processing query cannot be seven. It's a one or a zero, millions of times a second. Your choice about faith is not whether you believe or doubt, a one or a zero. Faith is a mixture. Faith is like the water from your tap. It's not totally pure. There's stuff in there. Always. Chlorine is some of the good stuff in the water, in the right proportion at least. Parasites are not. The question is whether the stuff that's in there, be it disinfectant or doubt, will keep you healthy or kill you.

~

When my mom began to show signs of aging, she would complain about floaters in her eyes, tiny particles or shadows that seemed to move around inside her eyeballs. I had no idea what she was dealing with, so my responses to her possibly weren't as sympathetic as they should have been. Floaters occur, typically with age, when the jelly-like substance that fills your eyeballs begins to develop imperfections, casting tiny shadows on your retina. I blew off Mom's complaints. But lately I've begun glancing up, sensing that something, like a cockroach or a mouse, is moving on the wall. But when I turn my head and look, nothing is there. Floaters. Heavens, I have become my mother.

There are times when God's presence feels to me like an eye floater. I can't quite make it out. I sense something is there, but it's just outside my focus zone. Is it real or is it an illusion, a mirage, a fabrication of my mind? What's causing me to sense God's presence as shadows? Is the problem me? Or is God not there at all?

The problem may just be my insatiable need for explanations, my compulsion to understand the cause and effect of any event or circumstance. Like, if I didn't ask so many questions, I might not have all these doubts, so stop! The older I get, though, the more I believe that the questions reflect the nature of faith itself. God resides in shadows rather than face-to-face. It's God's nature. God's presence and God's actions are not generally discernible. God simply cannot be irrefutably proven. Or debunked. That's the whole point. It's not that we can't find assurance of things we hope for or conviction about things we can't see,[6] but that's what faith is. In this regard, the opposite of faith is neither unbelief nor certainty; it's sight. And sight, after a while, is susceptible to floaters.

I will keep looking. In fact, I feel driven to look, to seek, to ask, to know. I think such longing for the divine is a mark of our humanness. I can't escape it, nor do I want to. Sometimes God's grace appears right in front of me. Sometimes it takes a little while for my eyes to adjust, but when I see it, I'm grateful. Usually, however, grace comes at me sideways. Unexpected, a little blurred. Sometimes I don't fully grasp it until after the fact, when I'm able to find some perspective. It's often later that I begin to wonder if I might have, in fact, encountered the surprising grace of God.

That hazy vision, blemished by floaters, or perhaps crawling creatures on the wall, may be because my faith, like my eyesight, feels shaded, obscure. It's sometimes clear, sometimes spotted, sometimes lighter, sometimes darker, sometimes comforting, sometimes troubling. Perhaps that's why I've always been drawn to the opening line of one of Gerard Manley Hopkins's most beloved poems: "Glory be to God for dappled things." That sentence has always bowled me over. I understand it, feel it, absorb it, live it. My faith is dappled, stippled, pied, brinded, freckled, and all the marvelous, variegated images Hopkins so wonderfully employs in his short poem.

I've never run from my dappled faith. I admit, however, that I haven't always worked to understand it or strengthen it or challenge it. Frankly, if I'm honest, I've sometimes worn my doubt-filled faith as a trophy. I have allowed myself to feel a little pride in being, in my mind, thoughtful enough and honest enough to have a faith that didn't require certainty—as if those whose faith is different from mine are dishonest or thoughtless. I don't want to be like that. I don't want to judge anyone else's faith. I certainly don't want my faith to be a thought experiment that I can cleverly manipulate in order to make an argument. I simply want to do better. I want to be a better person, a better disciple of Jesus. I suspect you do, too. When all is said and done, that's why I'm writing this book.

Fair warning, our journey here will not provide all the answers. It won't even ask all the questions. Like my faith, and I'm sure yours, the storyline will be dappled—shadows and light, shapes and patterns, hazy and clear. Our conversation here, like our lives, will often be nonlinear. Not everything in life is straightforward. Not everything can be put into an outline. Moreover, your stories and mine are not the same. Each person's faith has different stress points and strong places. I'm confident, however, that our experiences will intersect substantially enough that we can find in the hard questions a way forward, discovering new possibilities for seeing and knowing God.

We will begin our journey in the IF, in the uncertainty, in the questions: *If God . . . If God is here . . . If God answers . . . If I see . . . If I surrender . . .* We will seek signposts there that will both challenge and orient our quest. Then we will spend time in the WHILE, the in-between space—in the silence but also in the shouting, in the season between faith's struggles and faith's flowering, seeking a way forward that is faithful and productive. Finally, we will dwell in the FOR, asking about the purpose of our faith, seeing how our lives can become an opening so that others may glimpse God—not just somewhere out there but in us.

~

The moments just after midnight—in the confusion taking place in my own bedroom filled with medical responders poking and prodding me—were not merely an occasion for me to learn a few things.

The experience was certainly not fodder to write a book about faith. Notions of faith and doubt were not what I was thinking about on the quick ride to the hospital. This was my life, and I felt I was at a crossroads. But for some reason, rather than feeling fearful or overanalyzing mysterious and eternal things, I found myself oddly fascinated by what was unfolding around me. What did those medical-sounding words mean? What did the numbers suggest? Was my face still numb? Had I really slurred my words, or was my mind playing tricks? Is this a stroke, or have I overreacted? As we wound our way to the hospital, I listened to the banter of the attendants. They were focused on the business at hand, but they didn't seem overly concerned. So, I wasn't.

It was in the days after coming home that my thoughts began to turn to my own faith. Did God intervene that night? If so, did God change the course of my life? Like, would I have died if God hadn't intervened? I don't think so. No one in the medical community was scratching their head saying, wow, I don't have any explanations for what happened; that was a miracle. Or was God more interested in my faith aligning itself with God's concerns, trusting no matter what?

So, did my faith hold up? I think so. But some things are still unclear. At this point, I don't have a diagnosis or a prognosis. I think I'm going to be fine, but I'm no heart or brain expert. What if I find out it's worse than I think? What if my days are more numbered than I have imagined? How will my faith hold up? Will I trust God then?

These thoughts emerged from a heart not all that different from that of the nineteen-year-old talking baseball and faith to kids in the youth group on the banks of the Mississippi River five decades ago. The questions are largely the same, though my faith today is a little tougher, a little more resilient, a little more tender. That's what living does, what failure does, what doubt does, what grace does.

Sometimes I wish God had created a world in which God's presence was clearer, more straightforward, and utterly undeniable. It seems like it would be easier that way, though I suspect it would not actually be better for me or anyone else. Still, a word from God every now and then would be nice.

I listened to the paramedic sitting next to me as the ambulance approached the hospital. He was telling me about his church and the little business he had launched there, making T-shirts displaying the image of a cross made from strands of DNA. I'm afraid I wasn't paying a lot of attention. My mind was focused on other things, like whether I was having a stroke. A few days later, after I had returned home, a package showed up on our front porch. I opened it. There was no note, just a dark blue shirt with a beautiful artistic rendering of a cross made from DNA on the front. How kind of the paramedic. I was really touched. I just wish, you know, I had heard something from God.

if

If *reflects the unknown of our faith:*
If God wills. If God sees. If God answers. If God would only . . .
Doubt is faith's ***if****, faith's conscience. Its place is to serve faith,*
question it, and embolden it. Doubt keeps faith's feet on the ground.

01

LIVING IN THE "SOMETIMES" AND THE "SEEMS"

Every time I saw the large banner off to the side of the road, I felt a pang of discomfort in my gut. I could visualize the slow trickling of gastric juices drizzling down the lining of my stomach, like acid stripping the paint off a barn wall.

The sign was hard to miss. I know because I tried. It was spread across the front of the little church near where Lesa and I used to live. I would consciously drive different routes on my various city travels, even if it took several minutes longer, to eliminate the affront to my apparently fragile sensibilities. But I would inevitably forget, my mind focused on whatever urgent task was at hand, and find myself slapped in the face all over again. The banner offered this word of, I'm sure, well-meant hospitality to the neighbors and passersby: "Lost Sheep Welcome."

I often found myself wondering why I was so offended by it. Was it the "lost" part? Probably. I know what they meant. And I suspect that this church would have thought I was, in fact, lost, which certainly didn't make the greeting seem especially warm or inviting. Or perhaps it was the "sheep" part. Not a word I normally use to describe myself, though I get the allusion. Maybe it was the "welcome" part set so awkwardly against the implied judgment of both lost and sheep. Whatever the cause of my irritation, it just seemed so wrong. Or at least ineffective. Why would anyone whose moral character or eternal soul the church would have considered so depraved as to be called lost or whose intellect would be judged to be so stunted as to be called sheep choose to stop their car, pop into the building, and receive the promised welcome?

Perhaps the message wasn't actually intended to bring people into the building. Maybe it was an unartful attempt at image-building, like we love our neighbors, we love everybody, we want to be known as loving people, and we want all of you out there who are going to hell to know we care about you, and if y'all will come on in here, we'll do our best to get you saved because we know that you, dear sheep, are lost.

I get the biblical reference, of course. Jesus is the Good Shepherd. When one sheep is lost, the shepherd leaves the ninety-nine to search for the one. We care about lost sheep. We care about our neighbors. I'm just not sure that calling one's neighbor a lost sheep on a church banner opens the door wide for her to come running into the arms of Jesus. "Hey, Dorene, what are you doing Tuesday night? We're having a potluck dinner up at the church for all the lost sheep in our neighborhood. Hoping you might come."

Lost. The word settles slow and hard. It's a slippery little word, a lot like the word *love*. It can mean so much. Or almost nothing. I love my wife. I love potato chips. I lost my password. I lost my mother. I suspect we ask too much of these sorts of words. We ask them to carry more than they can bear. It's like pouring water into a tissue paper container. You can do it, but little of the substance will remain. When words lose their substance, they're not of much use. *Lost* has to carry a lot of freight. We should probably use it sparingly.

"So, you've lost your faith?" I've been asked that question at least a few times over the years. I think I understand why. For much of my adult life, I have found it fairly easy to refer to myself as a doubter. Not everyone understands, of course, especially church people, so I'm usually careful about how I talk about it. But I'm comfortable with the word, at least when I am the one who gets to define it. I'm a doubter in the "I believe; help my unbelief" sort of way. Jesus seemed to have accepted doubt like that without judgment.[1] Occasionally I view myself as the kind of person to whom Jesus might have said, "Go, your faith has saved you," but not all the time. Sometimes, I'm just not sure.

Frederick Buechner famously said, "If you don't have any doubts, you are either kidding yourself or asleep. Doubts are the ants in the pants of faith. They keep it awake and moving."[2] The operative word here is *any*, as in not having any doubts. No doubt I'm missing something, but I'm unable to grasp what it means to have no doubts, certainly when it comes to the will of God or the nature of the divine presence. One may be able to minimize doubt—to downplay it or wish it away or choose not to think about it, but I suspect doing so is less a triumph than a fundamental misunderstanding of God's nature and of faith. Doubt feels unavoidable to me, though I'm willing to allow doubts about that.

I have doubts, but that doesn't mean I've lost my faith. Not if by *lost* you mean misplaced or gone astray, like a coat or a soul. My faith is still around, sometimes visible, often alive and even urgent, occasionally the full "ants in the pants" version, moments uncommon enough to be cherished. I've never walked away from faith in God or even considered doing so. I still hunger for God and desire a full-throated, unwavering sort of faith. But God sometimes seems not to be present.

I live in the "sometimes" and the "seems." Sometimes my faith is strong. Sometimes I sense God's presence. But when I do, I'm always aware that God might just seem to be near, just seem to be in me. Maybe it's wishful thinking. Maybe I'm projecting my own desires. Or the desires of my long-deceased parents and other spiritual ancestors, reflecting a faith that mostly emerges from my upbringing. After all, my faith is somewhat like my parents' faith. And their parents'. Different nuances and different expressions, for sure. I'm not like them in many ways. But the scaffolding of my faith isn't all that different from theirs. So, is it really faith, or am I merely a product of social norming across the generations? And whatever it is or wherever it came from, what good is it if I don't feel it or cannot recognize it? How is faith useful if God is present only sometimes? And where is God when God seems not to be here? Or, at least, here with me?

A little perspective, though. My faith may be elusive at times, but that's not the same as faithlessness any more than distance is the same as abandonment. One is about time or space, the other about intent or neglect. But claiming such differences doesn't make living at faith's edge easier. Living amid the "sometimes" and the "seems" can be wearisome.

~

Not long ago, I was visiting a friend I hadn't seen for a while. I asked how things were going at work. A simple little question. More an act of social connection than an incisive probe into his life and circumstances. Nothing deep. You know, just finding some words to affirm our friendship.

In hindsight, I should have stuck with "How are you?" "Fine, and you?" "Fine." That would have saved me the theological root canal that occupied me for the next several days. But since leaving well enough alone is apparently not in my gift set, I pressed further.

"So, how are things at work?" Just an innocent question.

"Great. I changed jobs a few weeks ago," he told me. Here was the crossroads in the conversation, but I missed it. I could have stopped right there. I could have said, "How about that?" or "That's nice." But no. Just one more question to let him know I was fully engaged.

"Oh? I hadn't heard. What happened?"

"Well, a couple of months ago," he said, "I was sitting out on the back deck, and God told me it was time for me to change jobs. So that's what I did."

Whoomp! There it is. "God told me."

This is the hard-to-talk-about part, the part I sometimes struggle with. I don't know how God operates. At the same time, I have learned—or, as you'll see in these pages, I'm still learning—not to predetermine what God is up to. God can do what God chooses to do. So I'm not critical of my friend's response. I certainly don't disbelieve him. Truth be told, I'm a bit jealous. At the same time, I don't fully understand what it means or how it happens. I've never experienced such a thing. Not that I know of. Maybe I wasn't listening. Maybe I don't have the kind of faith I should. Maybe God engages people in different ways. But when someone talks about God that way, I have nothing in my experience to compare it to.

I understand the instinct to see God, to know God, to talk with God. I believe in prayer. I'm a person of faith. Much of the time. Or at least I want to be. But I also find myself puzzled or at least cautious. When the "God told me" part is spoken, the dialogue inside my head shifts into hyperdrive. My mind begins to analyze how such a thing could happen, what it feels like or sounds like for God to speak to a person. A sort of social paralysis kicks in. My brain fogs over. I don't know what my next words should be.

Inside my head, the conversation goes something like this: What should I say to my friend if the new job doesn't end up working out? Would that mean the message he received wasn't actually from God, or that God wanted to teach him some sort of lesson, or maybe that my friend didn't have the right kind of faith? If God wanted my friend to have a certain job, what then is God up to when other folks can't get a job at all? Why would God do that? Or why would God care about my friend's job, or my own job for that matter, when so many people around the world work harder every day than I do, have more faith than I have, and barely have enough food to feed their families? I don't disbelieve. I just don't know. Or don't understand.

Those are the sorts of questions doubt asks. They're legitimate questions, though sometimes they can lead to cynicism, a disease we once thought was incurable. Amputation sometimes works, though it can be brutal. Even then, it's possible for the cynicism to grow back. I know firsthand. At the same time, doubt keeps faith from sitting on its bum so long that it starts to cramp from lack of use. Doubt moves faith to new and sometimes uncomfortable places, where the push and pull of pain and recovery give our faith more strength and flexibility. But those aren't the things I generally say in the "God told me" moment.

What I say, and what I genuinely believe, is that I'm awed by that kind of faith. I'm humbled by the discipleship that says, wherever you want me to go, Lord, I will go. I love the trust that permeates that sort of faith. More than anything, I'm drawn to the sense that God is present, right here, right in front of me, loving me, making things happen, that the gift of God's grace is accessible, real, and for me.

I just don't normally experience God's grace this way. Grace doesn't typically grab me by my face and make me look. It doesn't take my hand and pull me toward the right door. I want to be in relationship with people who experience God's grace differently. I want to listen. I'm open to learning. I'm learning still. But when I discern it, God's grace usually comes at me off-center, from the edge.

I envy my friends whose faith seems abundant, lavish, bighearted, inexhaustible. God seems always close by for them, helping, making a path clear and navigable. I'm intrigued by that sort of faith, but I can't fully grasp it. For me, faith feels more like longing, like the heartache of someone in love, the aching to see her face or smell her hair, the yearning for the trace of fingers on bare flesh, lost in the memory of a tender embrace or the anticipation of reunion long delayed. Or faith can be like grief—a laugh or a whisper now gone, the remembrance dimming with the passing of time, the distance and the loss both more real and, distressingly, less heartbreaking.

But it is precisely the grief and the longing that make the consummation of faith so meaningful. If faith is like longing, I'm all the way there. If faith is about feeling the presence of God here and now, I'm mostly in grief. But that doesn't mean I don't know consummation. In fact, it is the remembrance of those intimacies with God, too seldom but always rich, that sustain my faith.

For some of you, such a struggle with faith may seem odd or even frustrating. When doubters talk about their faith, they can come across as unbelieving, even jaded. That's not my desire. But don't worry too much about doubters like me, thinking you need to shore us up or set us straight. We are not helpless. We can still make choices. We just can't fully escape the IF of our faith—if God desires, if God sees, if God is here. The IF is built in. And so, my mottled faith doesn't always show up, even when I desperately want it.

I may not always have faith handy, like a wristwatch that I can glance at any time I need to. Or like the phone I carry in my front pocket. Except for the time I lost it at a funeral. I didn't even know it was missing until after the graveside service. I looked for it everywhere. I even got down on my hands and knees, searching among the tombstones at dusk after all the people had gone, worried that I might appear to some onlooker like a specter looking for a purloined soul. I headed back to the church building and began to rummage around the pew cushions and hymnbook racks near where I had sat. Nothing. How do you lose a phone at a funeral?

Several days later, I got a package in the mail from the preacher at the church, one of my former students. It included no note, just my phone, carefully wrapped in toilet paper, dead as a proverbial doornail. Ah, yes. Now I recalled the quick trip I made to the throne room before heading to the cemetery. Mystery solved, but not the remedy to my embarrassment. So, I lost my phone. I have, over the years, lost many things—my keys, my glasses, my credit card, my dignity, my girlish figure, my charm, and, at times, my way. But I have not lost my faith.

~

Faith should have come easily for me. In fact, I thought it did. I assumed, like most of the people I knew growing up, that faith had something to do with going to church a lot. I got the going-to-church part down pretty well. My family was at church every week. Many times a week.

It wouldn't be fair to say, however, that I was at church every time the doors were open. On the contrary, my dad had a key to the building, which meant we could be at church even when the doors were locked, arriving early, staying late, and going pretty much anytime he needed to be there. Surely, going to church that often would incline a person toward faith. Or not.

I was about twelve, sitting with several of my buds, maybe seven or eight of us, about midway back in the sanctuary well behind our parents, who occasionally glanced back to make sure we weren't whispering or shooting spit wads or sacrificing a goat, whatever it is that twelve-year-old boys do, when one of us, several seats down the row to my left, started passing a note in my direction.

The game was "In Bed." The object was for each of us to write down the number in the hymnal of a song whose title would morph into a new meaning upon adding the words *in bed*. Do I have to explain the humor of twelve-year-old boys? The object of the game was to make us laugh out loud. The first entry to accomplish that would be the winner.

The initial attempts were a little lame. "It Is Well with My Soul in Bed." "Love One Another in Bed." "How Firm a Foundation in Bed." We continued to make our submissions, one by one, starting to get the knack of it now, passing the card down the row and back. "Abide with Me in Bed." "O Love That Will Not Let Me Go in Bed." "Rise Up, O Men of God in Bed." "O for a Faith That Will Not Shrink in Bed."

You get the picture. I'm not claiming any measure of maturity here. Or, frankly, wit. Just that my churchgoing wasn't a straight line to glory.

I don't remember who had the winning hymn, but that was never the point. When one of us began to turn blue trying to swallow the giggles rising in his throat; as tears began to run down the pious masks we had all carefully plastered on our faces in order to display to everyone around us the earnestness of our devotion; as, one by one, we would pick up Bibles from the rack in front of us desperately hoping we could find some verse in Scripture that could stifle our snorts and call us back to Jesus or at least restrain us long enough for us to gain a measure of self-control with the sober reminder of hellfire, outer darkness, and eternal damnation; when, at long last, the chorus of frantic coughs and faux sneezes could no longer conceal our unholy mirth, and every eye in the sanctuary had turned toward us, including the preacher's, whose piety did not have to be affixed to his face but apparently just grew there naturally—well, then the game was over. The ride home was quiet. Apparently, my parents did not share my sense of humor.

Clearly, not every trip to church enhanced my faith. Still, the faith community of my childhood formed me in substantial ways. I was surrounded by virtuous men and women. I learned to love God, to sing, to give, to serve, to care, and to pray. I preached my first sermon at age ten. It was actually more of a sermonette. About five minutes. On prayer. A box had been placed behind the pulpit so that the boys—and all of us were boys; the girls weren't allowed to speak in church in those days, spiritually scarring the kids, the parents, and the future of Christianity in general—could step up onto the box and peek over the top edge of the pulpit to see our parents looking at us so approvingly. Well, not entirely. My father, who loved my sermon almost as much as he loved the little boy who preached it, did remind me afterward of a couple of grammatical mistakes I had made. And my mom had been a tiny bit distracted as I apparently furled and unfurled my little tie through the entire ordeal, but that was after her hugs and her praise. All in all, it was a solid first effort. Church was good for me.

But church was also where I learned to doubt; where I learned the rules; where I learned to judge, to exclude, to condescend, to split hairs, to build walls; where I first knew guilt; where I first felt shame. But I never felt unloved. I never felt unseen. I never felt lost. Sometimes church seemed boring. Sometimes it seemed pointless. Sometimes it seemed trivial. Sometimes the questions seemed wrong, and the answers seemed contrived. And sometimes it seemed inspiring, empowering, mind-stretching, heart-bursting, and life-giving. Turns out, faith can grow in a place like that, among a people like that, perhaps superficially at first, timidly, unsteadily, occasionally smugly, in rare moments humbly, and in surprising moments courageously, creating over time, in God's own way, a sustained, compelling, consequential, thriving faith—in the questions and the doubts, in the uncertainty and the blunders, in the "sometimes" and the "seems."

02

WHEN OUR FAITH IS SIDEWAYS

Eccentric people are interesting to me. I've never particularly wanted to be one or to be known as one. But I've known about, or in some instances known personally, more than a few eccentric people over the years. My life is better, more interesting, more enjoyable because of them. I'm not suggesting that every eccentric person is worthy of imitation, but they do make the world interesting. Or they can. Eccentric people can provide variety and color but also a different outlook on things, new ways of seeing. They can be creative. Some of them change the world.

To be eccentric is literally to be "off-centered." The prefix *ek-* in Greek means from, out of, away from, or off. The root word *kentron* refers to the center of something. The derivative Latin word *centrum* originally referred to the fixed point of the two points of a drafting compass, the precise center of the circle. So, if centric is the point, eccentric is off point. If the center is the middle, eccentric is over to the side. Concentric refers to more than one circle sharing the same fixed point, and so to concentrate is to bring things together to a common center. Eccentric, well, not so much.

The English word "eccentric" was first coined in the early 1500s. It was a noun in the beginning, not an adjective. Its origins had to do with the nature of the universe. Everyone in those days knew that the Earth was the center of the physical universe. We had always known that. An Earth-centered, or geocentric, universe was obvious to anyone who had eyes to see. From where we stand, the sun, moon, planets, and stars orbit the Earth. We are at the center. Of course.

It had never been difficult to recognize that the sun, moon, and stars circled around us. Their paths seem direct and regular, around and around the Earth, year after year. But the paths of the planets sort of messed things up for the Earth-is-the-center-of-the-universe people, which in those days was almost everyone. The planets seemed to be going in their own little paths. From the standpoint of the Earth, each planet appeared to orbit the Earth but not in a straight line. Over time, they seemed to make long, slow loops, like distant curlicues, generally forward, but sometimes they appear to be moving backward, what medieval scientists and modern astrologists call retrograde.

By the 1500s, the church had accepted this geocentric universe as divinely created. Anyone who thought otherwise deviated from the truth. Eventually, some of those who did think otherwise were themselves deviated from the church, if not from life altogether.

One of the problems, however, with the whole geocentric thing was that by the calculations of the scientists of the day, the universe seemed to be in an orbit around a point that was not precisely where the Earth was. To explain how the planets orbited the Earth in loops rather than a straight line, the scientists of the day devised an ingenious solution. The actual center of the geocentric universe, they determined with as much mathematical precision as was possible in the sixteenth century, was out in space, some distance from the Earth. They named this hypothesized spot in space "the eccentric"—the off-centered point. That's when the word entered modern vocabularies—first literally, then metaphorically of people and ideas.

The eccentric was a singular pinpoint around which all the universe revolved, just a little way from the Earth. Off-centered. Since everyone knew that the Earth was the center of all things, mathematics could demonstrate the existence of this eccentric. It was the only thing that made sense. Until it didn't. And the world changed.

Dealing with changing worlds is part of being a grown-up human. The world as we once conceived it—what's important, what's right, how we view the reality around us—rarely endures all the years of our lives. At some point, we come to see things differently. More clearly, we hope. We understand new things. The center of the universe shifts. We thought we knew how things were, but it turns out we didn't.

We rarely see these sorts of changes coming. The beforemath to our world-shifting moments usually occurs over a long time. Throughout this unconscious, mostly invisible lead-up to significant change in our lives, we are processing new bits of data, new ideas, new questions, new relationships, new understandings. Our old way of thinking is being challenged, often imperceptibly. Our intellectual scaffolding seems to be the same, but our ideas and interactions are realigning. Those days may feel a little shaky at times. Things may seem uncertain or unclear, but on the surface our world stays basically intact. Until one day we look around, and everything is different.

Some psychologists call that moment of new awareness a gestalt shift, a seemingly sudden change in how we see the whole of things, what we know, what's important, what's at the center. We're looking straight ahead, walking down the road we've always been on, and then something grabs us unexpectedly from outside our vision. It seems to come at us sideways. New perceptions enter our personal universe, new pieces of information, new connections. And then things are never the same.

Turns out, planets orbit the sun rather than circling the Earth. The Earth is just one planet among many, in one solar system and one galaxy among billions. The Earth is not the center of the universe. And neither are we. The center was elsewhere all along. The eccentric wasn't just a little way out but somewhere altogether different. Way out, among the millions of galaxies. We just didn't see it. That's why, perhaps, eccentric ideas and eccentric people are often fascinating. They provide perspective. They reorder the forms and patterns of our minds. They help us reimagine our own world.

My all-time favorite eccentric person was my dad's mother. My grandmother Nell grew up in New Mexico several decades before it became a state. Her house was a dugout—a sod-clad structure built mostly underground—just outside the little frontier town of Roswell, which, much later in her life, gained international notoriety because of a UFO incident that supposedly took place nearby.

She grew up before the age of automobiles. As a girl, she helped her family make money by taking coffee and sandwiches to the nearby stagecoach station to sell to passengers. Because her home in her younger years was mostly underground, she required every house she lived in as an adult to have a basement, even if it meant having to blast through the bedrock in its construction. She simply could not sleep above ground. The smell of my grandmother consisted of two distinct odors—the musty scent of mildewed basement and the pungent aroma of ripe onions on her breath. She ate an onion a day like it was an apple. Every day. All her life. And more than one onion on good days. We did not always love to see her coming.

She had no qualms about doing things that others thought odd. As a young mother, she served her neighborhood as a wet nurse. I knew that story as a young boy. It was a while before I understood exactly what wet nurse meant and was horrified by the explanation. She prided herself on the volume and quality of her milk and regaled us with stories, quite matter-of-factly, of how she kept her milk supply up as if she were referring to keeping her sourdough starter active. What happened, we once dared to ask her, if there were no babies of her own or in the neighborhood to nurse? How did she, um, keep it going? Her one-word answer traumatized the grandkids for decades: "Puppies."

Her husband Jim, my granddad, was her cousin. Distant, I trust. He was small and frail. She was large—"big boned" as she called it—and strong as an ox. He was soft-spoken and gentle. She was outspoken and rough, at least around the edges. He was dignified. She was outrageous. He looked like an old man from the time he was in his forties. She didn't want to appear old, so her hair was always flaming red—dyed until she died at ninety-seven.

I loved my grandmother, though there was never a moment I wanted to be like her. I loved her drive, her strength, and her audacity, but I didn't want to move that far off-center. She liked being different. I like being liked.

Most of us experience pressure to fit in, to agree with the prevailing view, to accept the norms of our social network, our people. Outliers have their place, but it's not something most of us seek. It feels all right to be different from others if we're excelling at something. We like the best athletes, the best business leaders, the best teachers. But to stand out because we're "sideways" different or, God forbid, "below" different rather than "head and shoulders above" different is unacceptable to most of us. Few people enjoy being known as odd. Maybe unconventional or quirky, but not eccentric. Not too far off-center. Not that different.

Recognizing how each person's particular center emerged over time is part of what it means to gain self-understanding and grow into maturity. Knowing our story helps us reflect on who our people were, how we were raised, and what was important—which helps us understand why we see the world as we do now, why we act as we do, and how we see God, ourselves, and one another.

For me, at least in part, my center was formed around being reasonable. My people, my church, my denominational heritage emphasized knowledge, rationality, precision, information, and correctness. We were not the sawdust trail sort of Christians where repentant sinners came rolling or shouting or crying down the aisle to receive Jesus. Like many Christian traditions in nineteenth- and twentieth-century America, my tribe went to gospel revivals, except our people called them meetings to emphasize the thoughtfulness of it all. Our soul-saving responses didn't normally come with public displays. No weeping, cajoling, dramatic organ music, or other means of stoking emotions. Well, perhaps some cajoling. But our meetings, our sermons, our church services, and our Bible classes emphasized the reasonableness of the discourse. There are right answers to our questions. Any rational person can learn them. Make an argument. Change your mind if reason demands it. Weigh the alternatives. Make a good decision. That's how my faith was formed. Perhaps you can understand why I occasionally find myself skeptical, why I question things. I learned it on my daddy's knee.

The inconsistent part of this faith trajectory is that, for a group that promoted the rigorous pursuit of truth, there was a whole lot of certainty in our conclusions. Openness to truth wherever it might be found ought to lead to curiosity rather than certitude, humility rather than hubris. Truth seekers, by nature, should be open to a diversity of opinions as each one gives room for others to ask questions and seek answers. That was not my experience.

One of the consequences of these generations of Christians focusing on rationality and truth was the loss of any sense of the working of God here and now. The mysterious was marginalized. The truth and our obedience to that truth was our focus, perhaps even more than our faith in Jesus. I was taught the truth, clearly and definitively. The full extent of the things that were not known could, over time, be push-broomed into a smaller and smaller pile of dust, angled over into the corner where they could be ignored and, eventually, swept away.

This exposure to reason did its work on me. Rationality, when turned toward others, made me contentious at times. Turned inwardly, however, the commitment to reason eventually made me question reason itself. I learned to doubt what I was taught and then later to doubt my doubts. It felt good to run against the grain a little, to be out of step, off point, eccentric. Not too far, mind you. Not an onion-a-day sort of eccentric. Not full-blown peculiar. But enough for my doubts to germinate and produce fruit.

Obviously, not everyone who doubts comes from such a seedbed of hyper-rationality. There are doubters in every religious community. Some doubt because they were raised in a world thoroughly immersed in the Holy Spirit and aren't sure now that the Spirit can be either credited or blamed for all their faith experiences. Some doubt because they are the children of doubters or because their faith community focused more on outward rituals than on inward transformation or because no one in their childhood home ever expressed a word of faith. Some doubt because of the books they've read or the teachers who influenced them. Some doubt because they have faced difficult life circumstances—the onset of a devastating illness, the death of a loved one, the inability to have children desperately desired, the crumbling of a marriage, or the many ways in which faithful people can pray, urgently and earnestly, and feel their prayers were unheard, rejected, or ignored. In many ways, if we're honest, all of us are doubters about some things. Doubt has many parents. Its causes and consequences are myriad, not just in general but in each of us. What do we do when the path isn't straightforward, when the answers don't make sense? What do we do with a sideways sort of faith?

~

I sat at the back of the sanctuary, packed and overflowing, for the funeral of a girl who died in a car accident. I knew of her but didn't really know her. However, like almost everyone else in the room, my eyes welled with tears. The occasion was terribly sad. The music started, and the family began the procession toward their designated seats.

But the father did not sit. When he got to the front, he turned around and stood facing the congregation, waiting for the large family to file in. When everyone was seated, he began to walk back up the aisle, chastening the large gathering of mourners. Why is everyone so sad, he asked. My daughter is with Jesus. Don't cry. Rejoice. This is a time for celebration.

The room was quiet, unsure, supportive of the father and the family but a little confused. I had certainly never seen anything like it. Not too long afterward, the father cratered. His hospitalization was not brief. His certainty had collapsed, and no medication or surgery could fix it.

In another hospital on another occasion, I held the hand of a brilliant young woman who had given birth to a beautiful child, but the new mother had a damaged heart, and things didn't look good. Her devoted husband clung to their new baby as his wife fought for her life. And he prayed and prayed. But his young wife didn't make it. Do you blame him for being angry at God, for finding prayer difficult? Does doubting not make at least a little sense after such a loss?

I was a young pastor at the time of her death. My church family was reeling from loss. A respected congregational leader had cancer. He was getting better. A new treatment was promising. But then he died. A beloved teacher of the church's children got an infection. One thing led to another, and she died. And then one of the young children, the same age as one of my own, was tragically killed.

In my own grief, magnified over months, I had lost my words. I had no idea how to help these families whose grief was unbearable. I had no idea what to say to the young husband holding his newborn. I lacked the spiritual resources I needed. A friend encouraged me to read Martin Marty's book *A Cry of Absence: Reflections for the Winter of the Heart*.[1] The book grew out of circumstances in Dr. Marty's own life, the death of his wife, which had drawn him to the Psalter. Marty borrows and expands the powerful imagery from one of the twentieth century's most influential theologians, Karl Rahner, who used the metaphors of "summer" and "winter" to address two divergent and often competing expressions of spirituality.

The Psalter is loaded with songs of praise, psalms that Marty refers to as "summery spirituality." These psalms and that sort of spirituality reflect a life of summer warmth and abundant joy, rich in thanksgiving, acclaiming God's gracious and unending presence among us. These hymns of praise are wonderful, powerful, important, and needed. But they do not resonate with the souls of everyone and do not speak to every situation. Some believers express a faith that is murkier, permeated with doubt, whose experiences with God are not straightforward or chock-full of blessings. There are other psalms that capture those questions and that grief.

It was the texts for the wintry way, the laments, that Marty needed most. I had no idea how much I needed them as well. To my surprise, I discovered that the lament psalms in the Psalter outnumber the praise psalms. In our congregation, we sang a hundred praise songs to every, well, zero lament songs. I can think of none during those years. These laments were in my Bible, of course, but I wasn't reading them. As a result of this self-inflicted absence of lament, my feelings of grief and doubt had no grammar, no vocabulary. No wonder I felt inadequate for the task before me.

It became clear that I was ministering above my weight and was being pummeled by the blows. Too many of my parishioners were hurting, bruised by tragic loss and the sort of doubts that often arise in the wake of it. And more than a few of their fellow church members were trying to pep them up. Don't be so sad, they were saying. It's going to be okay. This is God's plan. All things work together for good.

My task in response was not just to address the well-intentioned but ill-conceived theology that often resulted in corrosive pastoral care; it was to choose helpful words or, better yet, to find a compassionate presence and constructive silence. These sufferers, at least most of them, were not having a crisis of faith. They believed in God and trusted in God's future. But their faith didn't look like that of their summery friends. About them, Marty says, "It may be that those who pursue the Spirit in unconventional ways, or who receive the Spirit's gift in ways that depart from those the group cherishes, receive no support. They are left to their own devices and, after frustration, choose to be alone again. Honesty is their premium, aloneness their price, absence their destiny."[2]

Communities of faith need both winter and summer. One is not superior to the other. Neither sort of spirituality is pure; there's always a comingling of doubt and trust. Faith, by its nature, is dappled, both for individuals and for the community of faith.

The souls among us who are naturally inclined toward a summer-like existence—for whom God is an "ever-present help," in the words of Psalm 46, even "in times of trouble"—are crucial voices of faith. Those of us who often walk the wintry way still find ourselves aching for summer. We need the warmth of the sun. We need you, even when we don't seek the sunshine. We may have questions about our pilgrimage of faith, a lot of them, and we may come across to others as a little out of sorts–off-centered, you might say–in our faith, but we're not ready to withdraw from the journey.

Be gentle with us. Don't cringe if we wintry sorts need to put on spiritual sunglasses. The glare of summer's spirituality can be awfully bright. Allow us to occasionally find respite from heated faith so that we can pray, reimagine, and, in time, reenergize. Grant us our tears as Christ himself wept, even though he knew his friend Lazarus would soon rise again.

Give wintry faith room. Don't fear it. Allow it a place at the table. Such faith can provide the sort of depth perception that only two eyes can bring, summer and winter together, looking jointly toward the journey's end. Winter travelers provide a needed perspective, reminding their companions that summer succumbs to fall even as winter gives way to spring.

Above all, let the winter Christians speak, but only when they're ready. Let them question. Let them challenge God. Let them ask the IF questions: *If God is present . . . If God hears . . . If God desires . . . If God cares . . .* Because in God's good time, the anguish of the IF makes the promise of the THEN more sweet.

03

IMMORTAL, INVISIBLE, HID FROM OUR EYES

The hymn remains much loved, four decades after it was first released, carrying to churches all over the world a sense of nostalgia and joy. It often begins simply, with a short piano intro, the fingers lightly touching the keys, gradually shaping the notes and harmonies that will drive this anthem. Let's start with a C chord—not the song's key, but the opening harmonic that will serve as the soil into which the song's roots can burrow. The melody in the right hand begins on a long E, then a light, quick E to F-sharp to G. Keep it soft. Don't be in a hurry.

The second chord is a G. Let it sit there for a moment. The congregation begins to stir. They hear it. They've got it now. Some begin to sway. Hands begin to rise. Then comes the D, a transitional chord that escalates the tension, pushing the music and the spirit in the room toward the E-minor, home base, an interesting chord to capture the powerful praise in the long crescendo that transports the worshippers toward the exaltation to come: "Our God is an awesome God . . ."

Sometimes the song begins not with a piano but with violins, or at least the strings mode on the keyboard, which provides a measure of depth, pathos, and a soft, understated beauty. Some days in some churches, it starts with drums, pushing the song hard from the outset with an unrelenting rhythm, which will meld with the chords and melody several beats down. Or it can begin with just the feet and hands—stomp stomp clap (rest), stomp stomp clap (rest)—reminding some worshippers, the Boomers most of all, of the opening beats of Queen's "We Will Rock You," a song that might actually work in this worship service. Except, you know, for the lyrics: ". . . You got mud on your face / You big disgrace / Kickin' your can all over the place."

But today the song is the Rich Mullins praise classic, which begins with these words: "When He rolls up His sleeves, He ain't just puttin' on the ritz, Our God is an awesome God . . ." Soon, the song breaks into the cherished chorus, repeated again and again—louder and louder, perhaps softer for a bit, then maybe *a cappella* for a phrase or two, then a key change and a new crescendo often with tears, cascading the worshippers into something resembling ecstasy: "Our God is an awesome God / He reigns in heaven above / With wisdom, power, and love / Our God is an awesome God."

Singing songs about being awed by God has been at the heart of Christian worship for centuries, though the modifier of choice has varied: Our God is an almighty God; Our God is a powerful God; a great and holy God; a good, faithful, just, infinite, wise, loving, merciful, gracious, glorious God; or, less poetically, an omnipotent, omniscient, omnipresent, immutable, impassable, inscrutable God. We don't usually sing about but may, from time to time, preach about a suffering God or a self-emptying God.

But we do not often sing about—or pray to, evangelize with, share on Hallmark cards, or prominently display in living room paintings—a hidden God. But that is our God nonetheless, though no whistleable melody or endearing chord structure pops into mind. Nor captivating lyrics—"Our God is a hidden God / Unseen here or heaven above / Remote, spurning power and love / Our God is a hidden God." Stomp stomp clap (rest).

That the God of heaven and earth hides is not a new concept. Nor is it some faddish rereading of the ancient texts. It has been there all along, displayed prominently in Scripture, not concealed, not camouflaged. We may not have thought about it, but once we see it, it's hard to unsee. Among all of God's attributes, the one we'd better come to grips with is that in the overarching biblical narrative, God in Scripture becomes increasingly hidden. How shall we understand this phenomenon, and what should we do with a God who hides? In the immortal words of Julie Andrews, let's start at the very beginning, a very good place to start.

In the opening verses of the book of Genesis, God is described as fully involved in the affairs of this newly formed world, particularly toward humans. God is tender and caring toward Adam and Eve, like any mother to her newborns. Or in this case, her newly mades. God breathes life into the man, then carefully crafts from the man's ribs the woman. The crescendo of this prologue of Scripture, written in the language and rhythm of poetry, moves from void to creation, from darkness and chaos to heavens and earth and every living thing, in increasing glory, to the pinnacle of the created order—first the man, then culminating in the woman. And they are, the poet exults, very good.

God then seeds, crafts, and nurtures a garden designed specifically for these children of God's own breath and hands. And, Scripture says, God was with them in the garden, speaking to them with intimacy and care, and they heard God's voice and responded. God was fully present, fully seen and known. God and humans would never again be this intimate.

A few chapters later, in the story of the great flood, God spoke directly to Noah, though there was no walking together in a garden. The whole earth witnessed the power of God as the lands were overwhelmed by floods. God made a covenant with the survivors of the flood, Noah and his family. Then a sign of this covenant was established between God and all life on earth. Shortly after, in the story of the great tower at Babel, God is again involved in the affairs of the world. Scripture says that "the Lord came down to see the city and the tower, which mortals had built."[1]

In these early stories in Genesis 1–11, often referred to as the Bible's primeval history, God is described as deeply and personally invested in the affairs of the world. But after Genesis 11, God's presence is never again made visible or audible to the whole earth, to all living creatures.

In Genesis 12, God makes a covenant with one individual, Abram, though it was for the benefit of everyone on earth. Later, when Abram encounters the divine presence, it "appeared"—a new word, a new concept in the narrative. God appeared not face-to-face but a step or two removed, as "a smoking fire pot and a flaming torch."[2] There are times in the story when God appeared to Abram as angels—not the magnificent, winged, European-faced angels of Renaissance art but, somewhat confusingly, beings that looked human and spoke in the third person about God but also in the first person as God. Later, Jacob wrestled with a man, or an angel, though he said later that he had wrestled with God.[3] The farther we go into Scripture, the fuzzier the whole God-encountering-humans thing gets.

God appeared to Moses as an angel in flames of fire from within a bush. God appeared to the Egyptians and the enslaved Israelites as plagues, sending signs as evidence of Yahweh's presence, and to the wandering Israelites by various appearances of "the glory of God," including manna and columns of cloud and fire.

In Exodus, God was still speaking, still being seen, but God's presence continued to diminish. In Joshua and Judges, the fire and cloud and the daily manna meals were gone. Occasionally, there was an angel or a miracle, but they were noticeably less frequent. Gideon, the judge and prophet, complained about God's absence: "If the Lord is with us . . . where are all his wonders that our ancestors told us about?"[4] Where have all the miracles gone, long time passing?

No other human saw God as Moses did. The last person God "revealed" himself to was Samuel.[5] The last person God "appeared" to was Solomon.[6] In the words of Richard Elliott Friedman: "The period of visible, audible encounters with the divine gradually passes, and not subtly, but rather expressly in the text. The people's hearing of the divine voice is not to be repeated."[7]

God had spoken to Moses "face to face," but in the days of the prophets, God's voice came only in visions and dreams.[8] Elijah battled the prophets of Baal at Mount Carmel,[9] and he prayed to God, calling for God to answer him. The answer was not a voice or a presence but a fire that burned up the sacrifice. This is the last public miracle in the Old Testament. In the very next story,[10] Elijah fled to the wilderness in fear. An angel, not God, appeared and told him where to go. Elijah traveled forty days and nights to Mount Horeb, the mountain where God's covenant had been given to Moses. There, brave Elijah hid in a cave.

The word of the Lord came to Elijah—in a dream? in a vision?—and spoke to him: "What are you doing here, Elijah? Go and stand on the mountain in the presence of the Lord because the Lord is about to pass by." And Elijah went. There on the mountain came a great wind, but God was not in the wind. And then an earthquake, but God was not there either. And then a fire. No sign of God. Elijah had come to see God, but so far nothing.

And then came what some translations call "a still, small voice" or "a gentle whisper." But these phrases imply something audible. The text reads literally, "a sound of thin hush." In other words, a sound that is not a sound. A sound of utter silence.[11] Elijah was sent to the mountain to witness the presence of God, but he heard and saw nothing of God. God seems to have pulled a veil completely over his face. So, Elijah pulled his cloak over his own face and went back to the cave.

At the cave, a voice said to him, "What are you doing here, Elijah?" Déjà vu. After Elijah offered an excuse, the voice told him to go and anoint a couple of kings as well as his prophet successor, Elisha. After this encounter, there are a few accounts of angels in other parts of Scripture, but no more wrestling matches with God or angels. No more fires from the sky. A few personal miracles but none that others saw.

We're just in 1 Kings. There are five centuries and more than two-thirds of the Hebrew Bible still to come. Why did God withdraw? There were years of exile, then a dramatic return to their homeland, to the ruins of Jerusalem, but there was no fiery cloud to lead them or manna to feed them. They seemed to be on their own. They rebuilt the city walls, but there is no indication that God spoke to anyone or helped them in any way. They rebuilt the temple, but there were no tablets containing God's commands to place in it, no ark of the covenant, which had always been the ultimate symbol of God's presence. The holy of holies, the most sacred room in all Israel, was empty.

Does this not seem somewhat familiar? To some of us at least? Most of the people in Scripture, Old Testament and New, never saw a miracle, never saw God's face or heard God's voice. We may wonder at times where God has gone or what God is up to. But even in the Bible, most people did not encounter God directly or personally. And when it happened, it didn't always go well.

The great hymn by Scottish poet Walter Chalmers Smith captures this sense of God's apparent absence: "Immortal, invisible, God only wise / in light inaccessible hid from our eyes." God was invisible. Why? Why had God hid?

Or maybe a different question needs to be asked, an other-side-of-the-coin sort of question: What else was going on as God grew silent? That one's not as difficult. As God's voice became quieter and rarer until it was a sound of thin hush, the human voice became louder and more assertive until it was a sound of thick hubris.

In their garden, first man and first woman seemed dependent on God to the point of helplessness. They did no particular work. God shaped the garden. Their only role was to enjoy it. When they took matters into their own hands, they accepted no responsibility for their actions. God banished them. They were naked and ashamed but were helpless to do anything about it. So, the Divine Seamstress sewed clothes for them and sent them on their way.

Noah seems to have stepped up a bit. He and his boys at least built the ark with their own hands. When the flood receded, Noah planted grapes and made wine. Each generation seems to take more responsibility. But why was it happening? Where was it headed?

Back in the beginning, the serpent had told the humans they could eat the forbidden fruit and become like God. The serpent was no fool; he had a pretty good sense of human nature. And that's how the story plays out, humans pursuing godlikeness, generation by generation. Abraham argued, negotiated, and made decisions, both good and bad, both self-serving and trusting. Abraham's nephew,

Lot, argued with a couple of angels, renegotiating the terms of his leaving Sodom. God agreed to the change of plans but said to Lot: I will grant your request to go to the town you've asked for, but hurry, "I can do nothing until you arrive there."[12]

God said, "I can do nothing." What? Not just God invisible but God impotent? This is not a memory verse I can remember from any of my childhood Sunday school classes.

The voice of humans grew louder, more self-sufficient. Humans aspired to be divine but couldn't quite attain it. God commanded, and they tried to obey. Sometimes. But then they failed, again and again. Jacob's struggles with God led to his new name—Israel, the wrestler with God—and the name was passed down to all his descendants.

Humans were made, in the words of one of the psalmists, "a little lower than God."[13] But a little lower is a lot lower than humans want. Something in human nature compels us to strive for more—to be like God, not so much in purity or holiness but in freedom and power. At our best, we grasp what we are losing. We feel God's absence. In the poetic language of Deuteronomy 32, God says, "I will hide my face from them; I will see what their end will be."[14]

We should not be surprised at God's hiddenness. The hymns of ancient Israel and the early church spoke of God's hiddenness often. Like,

> Why, O LORD, do you stand far off?
> Why do you hide yourself in times of trouble?[15]

Or,

> How long, LORD? Will you forget me forever?
> How long will you hide your face from me?[16]

And,

> Do not hide your face from your servant,
> for I am in distress—make haste to answer me.[17]

Amid all our troubles, God seems to have gone into hiding. How can that be? It's not that these prayers and poems reveal no mercy. God is not heartless. Isaiah, in God's name, offers divine graciousness toward us:

> For a brief moment I abandoned you,
> but with great compassion I will gather you.
> In overflowing wrath for a moment
> I hid my face from you,
> but with everlasting love I will have compassion on you,
> says the LORD, your Redeemer.[18]

How long has God's abandonment lasted? A brief moment? Really? From God's perspective, maybe. But from our own line of sight, it seems to have lasted a very long time.

But that was Isaiah and the psalmists back in the Old Testament. Didn't the New Testament address all the abandonment stuff? Surely the hiddenness of God was nailed to the cross, right? This is an important question. We will have to think further about how Christ impacted the divine-human struggle. But we're not going to be in a hurry. Let our conversation here serve as the prelude. For now, it would be helpful to simply acknowledge that the whole wrestling-with-God thing continues—not just before Christ but after, not just in general but in us. Someday we will understand. One day, we will see God face-to-face, Paul said. But for now, we see God opaquely, as though the glass between us and God were fogged up.[19]

We might prefer a world in which God is never distant or silent, where God's face is never hidden, but we don't live in that world. Christ's coming does not mean that we now get to walk close and carefree like Adam and Eve, hand in hand with God. Whatever intimacies we may feel we have with God, they're certainly not like the connectedness, the immediacy, the mutuality, or the closeness with God reflected in the original garden story. In contrast, God remains at arm's length from us. That sense of distance doesn't mean God doesn't love us. It means we need to let God be God.

Scripture is loaded with statements and stories about the extent of God's love for humans. The problem is our own assumption that true love must lead to constant intimacy, that if God loves us, God must surely be close, always nearby, like an omnipotent helicopter parent providing for our every need.

But there is nothing about divine love that rules out divine hiddenness. In the language of the theologians, God is both transcendent and immanent, both separate from us (the literal meaning of "holy") and near to us. The nature of transcendence is that none of the characteristics of God are fully knowable to us humans, including the hiddenness of God. This ignorance about the mind of God shouldn't call us to despair but to humility.

The reason Christ came, died, and rose again was not to undo the hiddenness of God but to confront and cleanse the arrogance, idolatry, and hubris of humans. That transformation is already within us, although its practical impact is still a work in progress. The intimacy with God that we long for is captured not in our sinlessness but in our hope, which requires us to wait and trust. New heavens and a new earth are coming, but they're not here. Not yet.

We shouldn't throw out our desire for divine nearness just because we don't fully experience it now. Our longing for intimacy with God fuels our hope every bit as much as our nagging doubts fuel our faith. There are things we can see, but our relationship with God hangs on faith, not sight. There are things we can know, but our future with God rests on trust, not certainty. Longing and doubt can be painful, but discarding them is self-defeating, like throwing away the keys to the kingdom because we can't see the front gate yet.

We can live every day fully within God's grace—free and forgiven—but God's hiddenness remains with us still. In fact, Jesus himself spoke of it—not in passing, not by inference, but directly, starkly, and at a pivotal moment in his life. In his greatest crisis, Jesus spoke about his own sense of God's hiddenness. How and why he did might provide the best perspective for understanding our own relationship with God, our own sense of God's distance, and our own cause for hope.

Is it surprising that in the last hours of Jesus's execution, the words of a hymn were on his mind? Jesus had sung hymns from the Psalter, the hymnbook of ancient Israel, all his life. One or another of the psalms seemed always to be on his lips. So, which hymn would Jesus have chosen to sing as the blood dried on his flesh, as a handful of his friends and family stood by, and as the bystanders gawked? It was hymn number 22. The twenty-second psalm. All thirty-one verses. Wait, all of them? That's a lot of verses. Jesus sang only verse 1. His death came moments later. But he knew the whole song. That's why he sang it at this moment. The hymn doesn't make sense without knowing how it ends.

If a song is familiar to you, when you sing the opening words, you know where it goes, you know how it ends. Sometimes, just the opening notes call everything to mind—the fingers lightly touching the keys—a long E, then a light, quick E to F-sharp to G. The words of the song begin with "rolling up His sleeves" and "puttin' on the ritz," but we know from the outset where it's going. And we know it's going to be awesome.

Jesus had been on the cross for hours. He was breathing his last breaths. He suddenly cried out in his native tongue. The bystanders ask, "What did he say? Was he calling for Elijah?" No, he was crying out the opening verse of hymn number 22: "My God, my God, why have you forsaken me?" Do you recognize it? Do you remember the tune? Surely, you know it by heart. You are human, after all. You know what it feels like to be alone, to question whether God is present. How long, Lord, will you hide your face from me?

My friend lost his job, but God does nothing. A couple from church has been wanting a baby desperately, but no response from God. God seems to have healed this family's aunt and that one's daughter, but not my child. Where is God, and what on earth is God doing?

We sin, I mean sin boldly; too much, too hard, too rebellious, too consequential. Could God ever forgive me? Can I find life again? Where is God in my time of trouble? Why is God hiding from me?

"My God, my God, why have you left me?" We sing it with Jesus now with a nod of recognition. Jesus knows. Jesus understands our predicament. It's been a while since we've sung it, but we're starting to remember. How does the song go? Oh yeah, after the decrescendo and the little *a cappella* part, the strings and woodwinds kick back in. Let's sing verses 27 and 28.

> All the ends of the earth shall remember
>   and turn to the Lord,
> and all the families of the nations
>   shall worship before him.
> For dominion belongs to the LORD,
>   and he rules over the nations.

God is in charge, the song goes. No matter what happens. No matter how grim it seems. We can have confidence in that. Now a key change as the trumpets and French horns join in. The tympanies thunder. Our hearts leap in our throats. Something is shifting. God is on the move. We know about God's absence. We know what it feels like for God to turn away from us. But God's hiddenness is not the final word. We sing the first verse in our heads over and over—why have you forsaken me, why have you forsaken us—but the song keeps driving us forward. Hiddenness is not the end. God has something else in mind.

It's not that God and humans can't coexist. We can. We can live together. We were made to live together, to walk a garden together, to break bread together. We just haven't been ready. We became the god we desired and found out we weren't enough. We aren't good enough, smart enough, powerful enough. Our own humanness has kept battling with the image of God in our own nature.

So, what does God do with that? What does God do with us? How do we find our way? We're driving toward the last verse. The grand choir now stands, their voices leaping into the swell of the instruments. The power of the music is almost more than we can bear. Each crescendo is overtaken by another, then another. Here is where Jesus's words, "My God, my God," were heading all along. Here is the climax of the hymn. Here is how the world ends, not with a whimper but with the sound of trumpets and tympanies and a chorus of praise:

> To him, indeed, shall all who sleep in the earth bow down;
> before him shall bow all who go down to the dust,
> and I shall live for him.
> All posterity will serve him;
> future generations will be told about the Lord
> and proclaim his deliverance to a people yet unborn,
> saying that he has done it.[20]

The final words of the song hang in the air. The whole earth is silent, leaning forward, standing on tiptoe, waiting. Will God hide his face from us forever? Will the veil finally be pulled back? Will there be deliverance, or are we abandoned after all? Can the gulf between us ever be bridged? Is there something, at last, we can place our hope in?

Jesus cried out again in a loud voice and gave up his spirit.

"It is finished."

He. Has. Done it!

Stomp stomp clap

Rest.

04

THE GUST OF GOD'S APPROACH

There's a song going around in my head that I can't seem to get rid of. It's more the lyrics than the music, but once an earworm burrows into your brain, it's hard to get the tune out of your mind.

It's not a church song. Not at all. But a country song. I must confess I don't listen to a lot of country music, so I miss out on a lot of beauty, not to mention social references to singers and lyrics. I have no excuse. I grew up in West Texas where authentic cowboys live and work.

Back in my high school days, the kids divvied up the dominant social groups in our school as "ropers" and "dopers." These terms weren't meant to be unflattering. Or even accurate. I was in the "doper" grouping even though I never did dope. In a few years, my friends and I would have been called "preppies," but that was after my day. I had friends in school who proudly wore the label "ropers." They actually knew how to rope. They had ridden horses and roped cattle all their lives. It was a fascinating world to me. It just wasn't a world I knew very well.

Several years ago, I spoke at a retreat in southern Saskatchewan, just north of the Montana border, about a hundred miles south of the metropolis of Moose Jaw. This is cowboy country. By the time I got there, it was clear that the retreat site was a long way from civilization. Everyone slept in tents and sleeping bags, except for the guest from the States. I was allowed to sleep on a bed with a mattress in the only cabin there. I felt bad about that. For about an hour. The weekend was memorable, sweet. These were good folks. Smart. Well-read. Dedicated. Fun. I felt comfortable with them because, as you know, some of my best friends in high school were cowboys. Comfortable until we started the trail ride.

I had been on a horse before. I mean, at least five or six times. My mom always thought I looked very handsome sitting in a saddle. I waved off the kind requests to help me up. Got on after three attempts and felt pretty proud of myself. Mostly my horse just followed the others, walking calmly without much need of my steady hand, until a herd of wild mustangs stampeded near us. I knew all about mustangs, of course, since I had seen them in movies. My horse wanted to run with them. I kept pulling back on her reins, telling her, "Stop. Stop." It dawned on me the next day that she might have responded better to "Whoa." At any rate, I was happy at that point to receive help from the cowhands who brought her back in line. I suspect it was somewhere about then that they started thinking of me as a greenhorn.

We had lunch out on the prairie, in a scenic valley nestled between two rangeland ridges overlooking a large corral where cowboys were working with a bunch of young male cattle. That's technical cowboy talk right there—a bunch of young male cattle. It's possible they referred to them as a cluster or a caboodle of cattle. I can't remember. These were Canadian cowboys, and I'm not fluent in Canadian.

It was castration season. I know there's a perfectly good reason for this harrowing procedure, but I wasn't sure what it was and didn't want to ask. I was mostly trying not to throw up. A bull calf, just a few seconds after the deed was done, was bawling. I didn't blame him one bit. I was feeling his pain. In fact, I was about to join him in the hollering when one of the women got off her horse and shouted, "Stop being a baby!" I think she was talking to the calf. My sympathies with the newly clipped steer were strong, but I heard the tone of her voice. I swallowed hard and kept my mouth shut. You've gotta be tough to be a cowboy, male or female.

One of the guys came over to me, castration tool in hand, and asked if I wanted to give 'er a try. The blood rushed from my face. "No, no," I said. "Hey, I grew up in cowboy country. None of this is new to me. I'm good." A few minutes later, there was a little burst of laughter from the guys, but I'm pretty sure it was just some cowboy joke.

The men and women I got to know that week were honorable, hardworking, and gracious. God was not just the object of religious devotion for them but a present, living reality. They talked about their faith with ease. They had no trouble seeing God in nature, in their work, in one another, even in me. One evening at the campfire, some of them told stories, and others sang songs. At one point, I grabbed a guitar and sang a John Denver song—more doper than roper—but it was the best I could do. I think of them often.

The country song I might have sung at the campfire somehow seemed inappropriate for a church retreat—"Looking for Love in All the Wrong Places." That's the song that's been worming around in my head. It was originally performed by Johnny Lee and was part of the soundtrack of the movie *Urban Cowboy*. "Looking for Love" was a number one hit for several weeks after the movie was released. The fans loved it. Catchy tune. Memorable lyrics. The chorus begins,

> I was lookin' for love in all the wrong places,
> Lookin' for love in too many faces.
> Searchin' their eyes and lookin' for traces
> Of what I'm dreamin' of . . .

That's what's been in my head. In many ways, it's the story of my life. Not that I'm looking for love. But I've been looking nonetheless—for meaning, for purpose, for hope, mostly for God. The search hasn't always gone well. God hasn't been easy for me to find. I'm pretty sure I've been looking in all the wrong places, looking for traces of what I'm dreaming of.

What *I'm* dreaming of. That's the crucial line. Looking for traces of what I think is important, where I think God is, and what I think God is doing. I'm looking right in front of me, straight ahead, keeping my eyes focused, making plans, marching forward, seizing the day, taking charge, serving the kingdom, seeking God's will, being strategic. My steady hands are on the reins. I'm leading. That way, I can go at my own pace and see what's in front of me so I can get to the destination I envision.

We humans tend to like what we like and search for what we desire, even if we don't know exactly what we want. Or whether it would be good for us if we got it. We're looking for traces of what we dream of. Our desires and needs push us forward. And sometimes God seems to show up. Or at least we have a certain feeling about God's involvement. A pang. A stab. Like whatever happened was too coincidental: Surely that was a blessing from God. Especially if it's to my own advantage.

Or sometimes, when we end up getting exactly what we dreamed of, we find ourselves disappointed. We prayed for a certain outcome, but the whole thing didn't work out at all. I've applied for jobs that I was sure would make a difference in my life, that would free me to best use my God-given gifts. I prayed, and the job offer came—or the move to a promising city or the purchase of a new house or a switch to a different church or whatever the big decision was—but it didn't work out as I thought. The whole thing felt like a setback. Or it ended up being terrible. Does that mean God didn't show up? Or maybe God was totally involved, but things don't seem any better, so what difference does it make whether God was involved or not? Or maybe God was teaching me something?

This is where the hiddenness of God can make things difficult. If God would only tell me what I should do, what decision I should make, I wouldn't be so headstrong and make so many bad choices. If I could get just a little help, then I would be better and do better. Didn't Jesus promise that? In his last conversation with the apostles shortly before he was arrested, he spoke about the *paraclete* he was leaving behind—the Comforter/Counselor or Advocate/Helper. In other words, God's Holy Spirit.[1] Shouldn't that be part of the solution? I believe in the Holy Spirit. I need the Holy Spirit. I experience, in fact, a measure of comfort that I can sometimes attribute to God's

Spirit. But not a lot of counsel. Couldn't the Spirit give me some good counsel from time to time?

But how do I get it? Where would I look? I've begun to wonder if the very act of looking might be the problem. Maybe it's just me, but here's how I often experience it: I need God. I desire God's presence. I'm searching for God. I have a sense of what God wants, what God can do, and how God might be able to use my stellar gifts and talents to bring about God's glorious ends. I just want to play my humble part in the unfolding of God's kingdom. If I get to play a conspicuous role, something that others see and love and express gratitude for, well, so be it. Just make me a servant, Lord. Amen.

Am I the only one whose search for God ends up being about myself? That's the flip side of God's hiddenness, isn't it? One happens at the same time as the other. As the human voice gets louder, God's voice pulls away. Or the more hidden God seems, the more shrill we become. Simple correlation? Or is there some cause and effect at play? Either way, in the sweeping saga playing inside my head, I end up being the lead actor and God moves over to the supporting role. Or maybe the stage manager. Or, better yet, the producer of the story—very important but working behind the lights, up in the control booth, away from the stage. It started off as God's story, but I ended up being the star.

As the plot of my life unfolds, I find myself again and again in a wrestling match about who's in charge and how it all ends. How does this keep happening? How did I become Jacob? Well, at least I get to play the central character. I can take some satisfaction in that. "Don't worry, Lord. I've got a good plan. You just show up on cue." But that's not how it plays out. It quickly becomes a power struggle, hand-to-hand, all night long. The crazy thing is, I often find myself winning the bout and getting what I want. Surely, that should comfort me a little. At least I can give God the praise. I can tell others what God has done for me, that God is good, all the time, that I am blessed, just, you know, out here giving my life to Jesus. What I can't figure out is why I keep walking away with a limp.

From that angle, the more we look for God, the less we seem to see. Or if we find what we're looking for, it doesn't always seem to be authentically God. And if we look closely, the God we often find looks a whole lot like the God we wanted all along, which is to say, a God created in our own image. We seek God and then worship the idols of our own making.

I recognize that not everyone participates in this search for God's presence. Some are preoccupied with other things. Some are caught up in the religion part—working the machinery of the institution, planning the future, restructuring the organization, making decisions without much reference to God's presence among us. Others simply don't care either way. Some would rather not engage God at all. Others are flat-out hiding from God. Like Jonah. Like me.

I know something about hiding from God. Not consciously. Not rebelliously. At least not in my mind. And maybe not exactly like Jonah. Thankfully, no great fish was needed to resolve the matter for me, though it was painful when God got my attention. Hiding from God, frankly, isn't all that difficult. Or rare. Most of us can live a long time without much thought of God's presence. We can be devoid of a meaningful life of prayer or discipleship, all the while going to church and engaging in public acts of devotion, serving God on the outside but still in hiding.

Surely, seeking God deliberately, purposefully, even aggressively, would be better than hiding. Hiding from God seems a bit cowardly. And on the surface, at least, a little silly, like a toddler who covers her head with a blanket and thinks nobody can see her. Wouldn't it be better to toss the blanket aside and walk out into the open? Wouldn't it be better to seek God than to skulk around pretending God won't notice?

I wonder, though, if it makes that much difference whether we seek God or put our heads under a blanket, whether we actively look for God on the mountain or hide with Elijah in a cave. There's a sense in which seeking God and hiding from God are essentially the same thing. We may seek God's face relentlessly, but as long as it's our show, our initiative, our plotline, as long as we are the ones lookin' for traces of what we are dreamin' of, then the search for God's presence is just another form of hiding. No wonder all that Elijah found on God's mountain was the sound of thin hush. Maybe the problem is not that we aren't finding what we're looking for, but that our focus has been on the looking.

~

I was in the library. Again. Hard hours dissolved into long days and countless months of wearying work. I was depleted. The work was not meaningless. It would lead to a worthwhile end. But there were some days when it felt almost too hard to bear. I was a graduate student working on my dissertation, and there was no end in sight. I had lost my motivation and my willpower.

After hours of pulling together obscure resources and long, boring readings about things that mattered only to the authors and perhaps their mothers, I found myself needing a diversion. I loved my studies, but in these dissertation days, to cite B. B. King, the thrill was gone. I just wanted a little time away from the pressing drudgery.

I happened upon a book one day in a section of the library I didn't normally go to. It was called *Out of the Silent Planet.* Hmmm. Science fiction. Maybe it's worth a look. Who's the author? I turned to the title page. C. S. Lewis. That took me by surprise. I hadn't known C. S. Lewis had written a science fiction book. I had read his *Mere Christianity* and *The Chronicles of Narnia*, but this book was new to me. I sat down at my study table and got lost in it. The science was dated, but the fiction was great. There was a second book in the series. And a third. I began to see the theological hooks he was setting. Fascinating. I needed more.

I found myself setting C. S. Lewis breaks—an hour at first, then two, and then over lunch and often the evenings. I was getting carried away. I had to set some boundaries. Each day I would make a covenant with myself: If you work for three hours without interruption, you may spend thirty minutes with C. S. Lewis. I often kept that commitment. I read *The Screwtape Letters, The Problem of Pain, A Grief Observed, God in the Dock,* several Lewis homilies, and Christian apologetics. I discovered *Till We Have Faces*, Lewis's retelling of the Cupid and Psyche myth, which pulled me into his academic work on literary criticism.

I found myself totally enthralled. I was seeing new things, thinking in new ways, somehow imagining my life differently. I had merely been looking for an escape, but what I discovered was the old thrill coming back. I found new energy, new motivation to complete my research and writing, even though his writing had nothing to do with my research. Then I ran across Lewis's semi-autobiography *Surprised by Joy*, and the pieces fell into place.

Lewis had come from a relatively religious family, though as he got older, his own Christianity became largely a chore. His heart was drawn to a different mystical impulse. From an early age, he was unusually fascinated by ancient myths, particularly the old legends of Scandinavia and Iceland and the Celtic myths of Scotland and Ireland, what he referred to as "Northernness." These stories nurtured in him a ravenous, almost insatiable longing, which he later called "a stab of Joy." But as Lewis grew into his teenage years, these experiences of Joy, these hints of the divine, became rarer and rarer. Joy had hidden from him.

At fifteen, Lewis rejected Christianity outright, declaring himself an atheist. Still, his desire to reexperience Joy remained. He missed it, longed for it, but he had lost the scent. Immersing himself in the Northernness no longer did the trick. Reflecting on those years, Lewis said there had been within him "the fatal determination to recover the old thrill," but "God had flown." These efforts to regain Joy were failures. He had nothing within him to make the object of his yearning return. In Lewis's words, "I had no lure to which the bird would come."[2]

He later identified two blunders he had made. The first was when he had begun to complain that "the 'old thrill' had become rarer and rarer." By so doing, he had made the thrill itself the object of his desires. The mature Lewis critiques his younger quest for Joy: "Only when your whole attention and desire are fixed on something else

. . . does the 'thrill' arise. It is a by-product."[3] The stab, the thrill, the Joy are not the main thing. You don't experience them unless you're looking elsewhere. They are glimpses of grace, but they do not come at you directly, do not grab you by the face to make you look. They come at you sideways.

Lewis's second error was attempting to produce the thrill himself. To seek it, take charge, make it happen. The harder he worked at finding Joy, the rarer it became in his life. He began to believe he would never experience it again.

During a season of spiritual desolation, Lewis fell upon some relationships and readings that caught him unexpectedly. He developed friendships with some young Oxford faculty members, believers, including J. R. R. Tolkien. He began to read the fantasy literature of the Scottish writer and minister George MacDonald, which touched him in ways he had not experienced before. And he discovered the essays, poems, and short stories of Christian philosopher G. K. Chesterton. In Lewis's words, "In reading Chesterton, as in reading MacDonald, I did not know what I was letting myself in for. A young man who wishes to remain a sound Atheist cannot be too careful of his reading. There are traps everywhere. . . . God is, if I may say it, very unscrupulous."[4]

Lewis's tongue-in-cheek toying with God's unfairness to atheists—God's way of "setting traps," of coming at a person in surprising ways—gets at the heart of things. Joy, Lewis discovered, always points away from itself, beyond itself. "[Joy] is never a possession," Lewis said, but "always a desire for something longer ago or further away or still 'about to be.'"[5] In other words, we don't possess Joy; Joy possesses us.

What Lewis says about Joy is what I experienced with Lewis's own writing. In surprising ways, these unexpected months of immersion in C. S. Lewis were a turning point. I hadn't been searching for Joy. I was just seeking distraction from the tedium and exhaustion of my studies. What I discovered was hope and life. I came for his stories. What I got was God.

There were God traps everywhere. I wasn't an atheist, but it was still the traps that snagged me. Lewis's language points to God not as the object of human searching but as a hunter, the one in pursuit. In the language of the classic Francis Thompson poem, God is "The Hound of Heaven."[6] From that perspective, we humans are not the seekers but the sought. Not the trapper but the divine prey. Thompson wrote of being aware of "the gust of [God's] approach," and he was afraid. Who wouldn't be? Even if it was a Holy Gust. Perhaps especially so. The hunter has drawn near. My heart races. The world around me begins to darken. Should I be afraid? God is a fearsome God, for sure. Or is my fear, my gloom, my dread simply, in Thompson's words, the "shade of [God's] hand, outstretched," reaching toward me, not to wound but to heal, not to harm but to touch, to lift, to caress?

Our choice is not between hiding and seeking. Both roles miss the point. The one doing the heavy seeking is God. The game, then, is not "hide and seek" but "sought and found." The greatest surprise may be that the God who seeks us rarely comes at us head-on and seldom when we're looking.

There is unexpected good news in the whole being-captured thing. If we are not the ones seeking God but the ones being sought, we can let go of some things. We can be free to relinquish our need to know what God is up to and why. Let God be God—generous and good but also mysterious and unknowable. Our job is not to control each situation or assume God has a specific task for us to do or a particular door for us to walk through. Look up. Look around. Be ready, not so much to do something but to receive something. Live with your antennae up. Enter each moment with a spirit of welcome, of anticipation. Then prepare to be surprised.

Lesa and I have a dear friend named Anne, an Australian minister and denominational leader. We learn from her every time we're with her. She's both humble and bold. Anne knows what it means to live with her antennae up. She recently told us a story about life in Australia during the 2020 pandemic. The loss of social opportunities was particularly difficult there. Anne began to ask herself, "Who can we help? What are the needs out there?" She began to pray for God to help her be present to what she couldn't see.

She went to the supermarket, just doing her everyday shopping, and walked past the flower section. A thought came across her mind: I should buy flowers for Lillian. The thought caught her off guard. Why did she think that? Lillian was her neighbor, but she didn't know her well. Nor did she know whether anything was wrong in Lillian's life. She didn't want to intrude. She decided to let it go for now. If this were a God-driven thought, she figured, then it wouldn't leave her. She went on about her business. The next day, the thought hit her again: I need to get flowers for Lillian. So, she went to the grocery store, bought flowers, and brought them home.

Anne said she felt completely ridiculous. How could she explain her bizarre behavior? What would Lillian think? "I hate being a weird Christian," she said to herself. "I had to stop and discern, is that my thought or God's? I never know with certainty. I have to work to get past my self-doubts."

She finally screwed up her courage and knocked on Lillian's door. When the door opened, Anne said, "Uh, so hi. I had this feeling that I should buy flowers for you." Lillian began to cry. She told Anne that these had been the worst two weeks of her life. On top of the pandemic, she and her husband had brought someone into the family business, but that person had betrayed them. They now faced the likely loss of their business and essentially all their life savings. Everything was at stake. Anne told her, "I'm a praying sort of person. Can I pray with you?" Lillian said, "No one has asked to pray for me before. Yes. I would love for you to." She told Anne she was a Christian and that she believed in prayer. And so they prayed together.

Their neighbors did, in time, lose everything and are having to rebuild. But they know Anne is continuing to pray for them. They've established a closer relationship. They now spend time in each other's homes for meals and celebrations. Lillian asked Anne and her family to come to their daughter's wedding. They talk often. Anne said, "Somehow, they became more than just people I lived next door to and instead became people whose life and challenges I cared about." She told me, "The biggest change that took place was in me. There is an increased level of warmth and connection. This story makes me want to be more sensitive."

Anne told me more of her own story. "I think God is up to stuff all the time that I'm oblivious to. I grew up in terrible circumstances. I didn't know God. No one in my family did. Then God plucked me out of one story and put me into a new story. My conversion story is basically this: If God is close, then I'm all in. God has changed my life. He has moved my life from black and white to technicolor." Now Anne is bringing color into Lillian's life. One day, at the grocery store, she thought about her neighbor and decided to buy her flowers. She didn't need to know why. It didn't matter where the nudge came from. She was just living with her antennae up. The antennae detected something, and she acted.

C. S. Lewis said that in his later years, he didn't spend a lot of time thinking about the old thrill. He still felt Joy, but he didn't place as much significance on the experience of it. "It was valuable," he said, but "only as a pointer to something other and outer." When we are lost in the woods, Lewis said, the sight of a signpost is priceless. "He who sees it cries 'Look!' The whole party gathers around and stares. But when we have found the road and are passing signposts every few miles, we shall not stop and stare."[7]

You become more comfortable with the signposts. It's not that you take them for granted. You remember the unexpected longings, the unsought burn of being, the insistent, persistent gravity, and the unanticipated glimpses of God. You still might experience a pang of gratitude, remembering with joy the first signposts you saw back a few miles when you were still lost. But no need to gawk or linger. The signposts are not what you're looking for. The destination is not here. Home is up ahead.

while

*To live in the **while** is to listen for God when God seems hidden.*
***While** is living now, here, fully present,*
but also not yet, someday, in anticipation.
*Embracing the **while** will mean learning how to be silent,*
because silence provides the space and the power to hear and,
when the time is right, not just to speak but to shout.

05

THE COMMA BETWEEN NOW AND HOME

We have dwelt for a time in the IF. If God. If God hears. If God answers. If God abandons. If God seeks. If I hide. If I wait. If I'm lost. If I'm safe. If I don't know. If I trust. If it is winter. If it is hard.

Doubt inhabits the IF like silence inhabits a song, not always noticeable but always near, providing context, anticipation, rest, and meaning. Doubt is not the enemy of faith any more than winter is the enemy of summer. One flows from and into the other—fallow becoming pasture's seedbed, flowering becoming pasture's compost. The gift is to see doubt, like winter's ground, not as faith's end but as faith's soil for emergence and promise.

Doubt does not surrender to faith, as if a strong faith finally wrestles doubt into submission. The I-don't-know and the I'm-not-sure keep faith on its toes, enlivening its imagination, extending its reach, expanding its depth. But doubt also keeps faith humble, reticent to judge or to revel in its own glory. Doubt nurtures faith—ignites it, shapes it, matures it, elevates it, limits it, animates it, admonishes it, cultivates it, and gives it courage. Doubt nudges faith to ask, inspires faith to seek, empowers faith to knock. How else will we know if the door is open?

Our challenge here is not to resolve the IF. Attempting to do so would be both foolish and futile. Rather, we will be seeking perspective and clarity to live in the WHILE.

WHILE is an in-between word. It's largely a term of duration in modern English. It refers to the time between some action or event that came before and a new thing that is still to come: "Lindsay put plugs in her ears while her son practiced the violin." While. Just for a time. The screeching will end soon. The earplugs are not forever. But in between, decisive action is called for. Or when circumstances require it, patient waiting.

But the roots of WHILE are deeper than duration. They go back through Old Saxon, Old German, and Old Norse to the word's Proto-Indo-European origins, meaning "to rest, to be quiet." In the beginning, WHILE was silence.

~

There are some churches where being quiet is the norm, where you enter in silence, kneel in silence, pray in silence. Songs are sung and sermons preached, but there's not a lot of chatter in the room. Wait to visit, please, until our time of fellowship, when you will find coffee and finger foods in the vestibule.

My church growing up was more of a chatter church, at least before and after the services. The powers-that-be at the church once decided that silence would show more reverence to God, so they put signs in the foyer, "Be Quiet as You Enter." Didn't really work. The problem wasn't so much the row of twelve-year-old boys plotting mischief but the old men down front, including my grandfather. My quiet, gentle-spirited granddad was deaf as a post. He and his aurally challenged friends would shout greetings and pleasantries at each other in the minutes before the service started.

"Is your wife here?"

"Yes, she can hear."

"No, not 'hear.' I mean 'here.' Is she present at church today?"

"Don't give it to her here. If you have a present, just bring it to the house."

"I know she's your spouse. I was just asking if she's here."

"Yes, she can hear."

The worship leader would wait patiently as the wives tugged on their husbands' arms and ushered them to their seats. The "Be Quiet" signs lasted less than a month.

Even though the churches throughout my life had been relatively noisy places before and after the services, it was usually quiet once things got underway. Not a lot of shouts of "Amen." No moving around of kneeling benches, which no one thought we needed anyway. Prayers were typically nonchalant affairs, each person perched casually on the pew like we were making small talk with the neighbor on the other side of the fence. It's just a prayer. No need for, like, you know, fear and awe. There was singing, of course, but everything else came from the pulpit. Quiet, casual listening was the default.

That was then. My new church in my new city was different. It was a talk-back church, a call-and-response church. Lesa and I loved the exuberant worship, the noisy two-minute greetings that always ended up taking fifteen minutes or more as we talked and hugged and danced and shouted while the praise band played. We hardly ever thought about being the only white members of a Black church. These were our brothers and sisters, our family, our closest friends in the city. The services and these people shaped us in profound ways.

The sermons from the senior pastor, my long-time friend, were intense affairs—brilliantly conceived and executed, engaging, informative, sometimes funny, often poetic, always deep. It was precisely because he preached to a motivated and energetic congregation that a well-timed moment of silence could be devastatingly effective. When it happened, you knew his next words were going to be compelling.

On this Sunday, in this sermon, his silence seemed interminable. Almost physically painful. It was not an awkward silence, like he had forgotten what to say next. He was holding the silence with his eyes, prolonging it with purpose, until some of us began to squirm uncomfortably in our seats. But the next word was not his. It belonged to one of the sisters down the row. Her word, as much a question as an exclamation, hung in the air for a moment: "Well?"

The first time I ever heard this response from a member, I found it a little confusing. In the churches I had been a part of, I had encountered an occasional "Amen!" but there was no "Well?" ever to be heard. I wasn't sure, at first, what it meant. But over time, the "Well?" began to make sense. It's raised as a question, voice rising, but it's intended as a term of encouragement, both to the preacher and to the congregation. It's part of the dialogue of a church where preaching is not unidirectional from preacher to congregation but is shared by the whole church. We all owned the sermon. We all participated. We didn't set the sermon's direction, but we could affect its flow and occasionally stir it up.

The "Well?" our sister spoke that Sunday was not meant as an intrusion on the sermon or an expression of discomfort in the long pause but a participation in the message itself. It was a word to the preacher to lead on, to lift the church up, to take us higher, farther, deeper, to draw us into God's powerful presence. It was also a word to the congregation to step up, step in, step forward, grab the silence, and turn it into action. Voices all over the sanctuary began to join her spoken word: "My, my!" "Yes, Lord!" "Lead me, Lord!" "Preach!" It had been what our pastor was waiting for. He had led us to this moment.

~

I do not and cannot speak for Black churches. I want to be clear about that. First, predominantly Black churches, like predominantly white churches, vary from congregation to congregation and denomination to denomination. Churches may share traditions, instincts, and behaviors, but no congregation is the same as any other.

More important, I do not know what it's like being Black in America. Period. A lifetime with all the advantages of being white simply does not allow me to comprehend fully. I do not pretend to know and do not intend to caricature Black churches or Black culture. I do know, however, what my particular congregation was like. I was immersed in it for almost five years. For two of those years, I served, unexpectedly, as an executive pastor. And I'm aware of some common threads among some predominantly Black congregations. I have had many conversations and have read extensively from ministers and scholars about Black preaching and worship. My life has been enriched by it.

In that light, Evans Crawford provides a valuable description of the congregation-and-preacher dialogue common in Black preaching. He lists five frequently used responses, a sort of hierarchy of congregational expressions or exclamations that start, sustain, encourage, heighten, emphasize, and crown a call-and-response sermon.

1. "Help 'em Lord!" is a search for connection, an anticipation of direction and prayer.
2. "Well?" is a hint to the witness, a celebration, a call for escalation of the rhetoric, a shared riff with the preacher and congregation.
3. "That's all right!" suggests possibility, the raising of the narrative toward Good News.
4. "Amen!" affirms the truth now spoken and heard; the pitch is right for the people and for their reception of the Good News.
5. "Glory Hallelujah!" is the point of loudest praise, highest joy, shared wonder, personal commitment, and congregational thanksgiving for the working of God.[1]

We generally live our lives, all of us, in the "Help us, Lord!," the "Well?," and the "That's all right!," in the regular, God-infused humdrum of the day-to-day. I'm not sure we could bear the floodlight of perpetual "Amen!" and "Glory Hallelujah!" The "Well?" is what keeps us walking in faith. It thrives in the WHILE, the in-between, where God's presence may be subdued but still desired. The "Well?" pushes our modest faith forward when the end is not clear, when God's word seems muffled, when my faith is as deaf as a post, when I can't hear even when I hear. The church's "Well?" is a reminder that God's voice may not always be audible. But if we lean forward a little, sit still long enough, and listen, we may be able to get wind of it—not in a repeated sounding joy but in the still space, not just in the thunder but in the thin hush.

~

The Japanese call it *ma*. In English, the word is usually translated "space," but like most translations, no single English word is exactly right. In Japanese aesthetics, *ma* is the negative space in a painting or a silence in a play or an empty space in a garden or an arrangement or a home—except the emptiness is not truly empty. The space is created to draw the eye or the ear. It has purpose and impact. It frames or highlights the beautiful. It provides balance, a counterweight. It is as valuable in the setting as the object it defines. It doesn't just emphasize the beauty; the space itself is beautiful.

In Japanese tea ceremonies, the setting of the table has precise rules. Space is divided into imaginary lines on which objects are arranged. The most valuable object on the table must be set along the centerline but not in the very middle. It must be off-center. This gap between the center point and the object's placement is the *ma*. It's not so much the absence of something but the heart of the arrangement. Done well, the space, the distance from center, may even cause one's soul to ache.

For that reason, "space" may not be the best translation. "Space" in English draws attention to the emptiness. A better word might be "place." Place signifies something more substantial, a presence more than an absence. It offers balance, memory, even yearning. The off-centeredness of the *ma* in a painting or a garden or a play is the element of nonperfection leaning toward or hinting at that which is perfect or complete. It doesn't stand apart from perfection, simply pointing to it, but it participates in it, nudging the observer into the perfect more fully.

Doubt is the *ma* of faith. Doubt is not separate from faith but is essential to its nature and its beauty. Doubt is not faith's opposite but faith's partner. Without doubt, faith is nothing but sight, and so we end up blind to faith's purpose and power. Doubt is what makes faith faith. Doubt may sometimes be experienced as emptiness, but doubt itself is not empty. Doubt has substance. It is the place where questions can be asked, where memories can be stored, where longing can be treasured. It is the place where a fist can be raised toward God or hands lifted in confusion or frustration, where a shout of "How long?" or a query of "What?" or a whisper of "I'm in trouble" may be uttered. It is a place of wrestling but also of safety. It is the place where God may confess, "I abandoned you for a brief moment, but with great compassion I will gather you back."

Doubt is the comma that separates faith's words and clauses, the *ma* in a clause or a sentence that provides location and perspective—like the pause between grace and sideways, between the source of God's generosity and the unexpected trajectory from which that generosity flows. It is the small break in a flow of words that allows the viewer to stop, to reorient, to reflect on the word or phrase just read and to anticipate the one yet to come. It is a marker between words or a series of words, little spaces—miniature signposts, if you will—that provide understanding, balance, and meaning.

Commas are a relatively new invention. In classical times, there were no spaces between words, no punctuation marks. The writing was *scriptio continua*, one letter after another, all capitals, no spaces. Consider the following two sentences:

GREETASYNCRITUSPHLEGONHERMESPATROBASHER
MASANDTHEBROTHERSANDSISTERSWHOAREWITH
THEMGREETPHILOLOGUSJULIANEREUSANDHISSISTER
ANDOLYMPASANDALLTHESAINTSWHOAREWITHTHEM

Simple, right? You know every word. Well, there are a couple of names that might not be familiar to everyone. The sentences are from Paul's closing salutations to the house churches in Rome. Imagine page after page of script like that. Ancient scribes copied these manuscripts, one letter at a time, no periods or commas, words split at the end of lines to save space, all the way to the end of the letter or document. The interpretation of the document would generally be left to someone in a higher social class. For the scribe, it was just letter after tedious letter. An orator might make some marks on the page to help in the delivery of a speech but no marks for grammar or for deciphering a sentence's meaning. No one read a document at first sight. It took time to unlock the puzzle of letter upon letter.

Around a thousand years ago, scribes and scholars began to introduce a system of markings to facilitate their reading, which eventually became modern periods, colons, and commas, mostly standardized after the invention of the printing press. In some ways, punctuation has remained fluid until contemporary times. Some of us are old enough to remember typewriters that did not have a key for an exclamation point. (Because of the massive overuse of this keystroke in our social-media-driven world, not having exclamation-mark keys might be a welcome thing!!!) Mid-twentieth-century typewriters, as your grandparents could tell you, were able to do a workaround to create this oughta-be-marginal punctuation: type a period, then backspace, then type an apostrophe. Thankfully, winky-face emojis had not yet been invented! ;)

Reading would be impossible without spaces, punctuation, and, of course, the letters themselves. These markings and blanks offer the clues we need to understand. They provide a sort of grammar, a visible structure of symbols and spaces that create a framework of meaning, every bit as important as the grammar embedded in the language itself.

The grammar of faith is saturated with doubt. Faith can hardly be understood apart from the markings and spaces, the symbols and punctuation, the semicolons and exclamation points that doubts supply. They provide faith not just structure but direction and thrust. Doubts are the commas, the *ma*, the "ants in the pants" of faith. Without doubts, faith is limited, thin, at least partly blind, and very possibly dead.

~

Cardinal John Henry Newman famously said, "To live is to change, and to be perfect is to have changed often."[2] Change happens. Not just in life but in meaning—the meaning of words, the meaning of ideas, the meaning of faith. Meaning changes because communities change, because culture changes.

Words change meaning over the centuries. Sometimes since breakfast. "Nice" used to mean silly. "Silly" used to mean innocent. "Pretty" used to mean cunning. "Bully" was a sweetheart. "Naughty" was someone who had nothing. "Bad" used to mean, well, bad. "Egregious" meant exceptional. "Fizzle" meant passing gas quietly. "Sick" used to mean unwell, like someone fizzling egregiously.

One's community provides a context for understanding because meaning changes not just over time but across groups. Words are social constructs. In the language of the old axiom: Words don't mean; people mean. That's also true of silence. As a white Christian in a Black church, my understanding of some things had to change. I had to see the world differently because the world was different. My world was different. When my understanding changed, my faith changed, which opened up for me new ways of discerning God's presence.

In the years before joining this faith family—where talking back and shouting were common, and occasionally falling on the ground in spiritual despair and desperate prayer—I had been immersed in the language and practice of quiet contemplation and solitary spirituality. Those disciplines hadn't come easily for me, but the practices were important, as much as anything, because a lot of people were doing them, and I didn't want to be left behind. But I also hoped these practices would help me address my doubts more beneficially. They would enhance my praying, my listening for God.

Through those years, contemplation and meditation were essentially synonymous. I learned the postures and language of Christian meditation and prayer. I learned about Ignatian spirituality, such as prayers of desolation and consolation and the grace of holy indifference. I devoured the writings of Richard Foster and Dallas Willard. I learned about the spiritual disciplines of simplicity, meditation, fasting, submission, and especially silence and solitude. I believed in it and still do. They are life-forming. I was learning that silence and solitude are at the heart of Christian spirituality. But I was not particularly good at it. I did not love it. However, I came to believe that learning spiritual disciplines, especially silence and solitude, were critical to my ability to discern God's presence. I still think that's right.

But in my new church, I came to see a different sort of spirituality, a different understanding of contemplation, a different sort of seeing God. My first Sunday at the church was the day after the George Zimmerman verdict. The slaying of Trayvon Martin had shaken the nation. For many Black Americans, it struck a resonant chord of familiarity. If you were Black, you could get killed just for walking to a store to buy Skittles. The only church members I knew that Sunday morning were the pastor and his family. Others greeted me warmly, but they didn't know the white guy. I felt conspicuous, a little out of place, in ways that every person in that congregation experienced every day in a world dominated by white people, something I came to understand only later.

The songs that morning were stirring—praiseful, poignant, ascendant, captivating. The sermon was riveting. "We are hurting today. We have a right to be in pain. We have a right to cry for Trayvon. We do not believe justice was done in this verdict, but justice does not belong to us. We are not George Zimmerman's judge. That's God's job, not ours. God calls us, in our pain, to love anyway, to love others anyway, to love our enemies anyway." The sanctuary was filled with the shouts and cries of a people hungry for healing, for the mercies of God.

At the end of the service, five young boys, children of the church, performed a liturgical dance as a music video played behind them, a song about children imitating their father, about God's children imitating our Father. I could hardly breathe. Everyone was standing and shouting. I watched the sorrow in the room being baptized by joy, their immense grief by a flood of gratitude. Something holy was taking place.

On that day, I arrived as a stranger, but by the end of the service everyone in the room had hugged me. When I left, more than three hours after I had come, I knew two things: First, I was going to have to rethink what spirituality was. Second, I knew I was home.

Barbara Holmes, the theologian, minister, attorney, activist, and scholar of spirituality, has written extensively about the contemplative practices of the Black church. In her compelling book *Joy Unspeakable*, Holmes describes the pull of silence on Christian spirituality, especially those whose spiritual practices were of European descent. She recognizes the value and power of silence and never criticizes silence as a source of spiritual renewal: "Those who study contemplation have assumed that the difference between European and Africana approaches to contemplation is the presence or lack of silence. This distinction could only be made in the modern era, as historically silence was interwoven in both traditions. Although silence is not necessarily the focus of contemplation in Africana, it is always part of the human experience."[3]

Silence is neither the solution nor the problem. To be human is to be silent or know seasons of silence—or to be silenced. Holmes continues, "We tend to presume that one must create silent spaces for contemplation,"[4] as if the only way to contemplate the divine is quietly and alone. That's essentially what I was taught, what I had come to believe. For the distant ancestors of most Black Americans, however, silence was not self-created but was imposed by their colonial masters. Their singing and dancing were crushed into a repressive, stifling, suffocating hush, a collective remembrance of voices forcibly silenced, a wound passed down from generation to generation.

Silence is inevitable. For all of us. It's common to the human experience. We are born out of silence. We die into silence. For some of us, Holmes says, silence can "fully envelop and nurture our seeking." But that's not true for everyone. Silence is not the only soil for the renewal of our faith, not the only voice to call us into God's presence. "Others," Holmes says, "who have been silenced by oppression seek to voice the joy of spiritual reunion in an evocative counterpoint."[5] Giving a full and sometimes thunderous voice to that joy of spiritual reunion disrupts the silence and transforms it.

A noisy, boisterous community discipline of contemplation seems out of place to many white Christians, but it is, nonetheless, true, godly, and spiritually forming. For those believers, spiritual growth often emerges not in silence and solitude but in shouts and dance, in tears and wails, in jubilant, sanctifying, caring, sacrificial community—the presence of God embodied in the public witness of the people of God.

My previous desire to know God through the means of silence and solitude was not misplaced. The instinct was, and still is, good and right. But it also emerges from a certain trajectory. It reflects, at least in part, a European-formed spiritual instinct. For quite some time, that impulse was cultivated in the domination and subjugation of its colonial victims. The tragedies of that difficult period do not undercut the vital importance of these contemplative practices, which long precede those years of oppression and which remain transformative for the people of God.

But the descendants of the victims of that subjugation now have something to say. I have come to believe that the community-soaked, noisy, fully embodied spirituality that is common within the Black church is not simply an alternative to the more individualistic, inward, and silent sort of spirituality. Rather, it's an extension and a corrective. Both sorts of spirituality nourish our faith. Both are disciplines of deep, life-changing contemplation. Both provide ways of seeing and knowing God. They feed each other. And need each other.

~

The silence in the sermon that morning was almost overwhelming. The seconds felt like minutes. But a word hung in the silence, just out of reach. I did not yet know this word. Only its form and sound, not its power. I could not possibly have latched hold of it or spoken it. I did not know it fit here. I did not yet know the language of God that was interwoven within the hearts of these people. My doubts had been heavy. God's hiddenness in my life had been acute. My silence was weighing me down.

But our sister knew the word. She spoke, not with a shout but still boldly, offering the one-word question, which was also an encouragement and an exhortation. The word spoken was not an individual act but a shared riff, not an end in itself but a perfectly placed comma that kept one hand holding onto now as the other hand reached toward home. The accompanying shouts of my brothers and sisters began to rain down God's glory upon our heads. "My, my!" "Yes, Lord!" "Lead me, Lord!" "Preach!" The church had caught the pause and the holy word from the pew and then pushed it toward the "Amen!" Before long, this family of faith, even the doubters, were able to say, by shouts and in silence: "Glory Hallelujah!"

From the soil of the winter comes the possibility of new pasture. Out of thin hush, arises a small seedling of hope.

"Well?"

06

BENEATH THE WOW AND AWE

It can be hard living in the WHILE, between God's hiddenness and God's intimacy, between the silence and the shouts, between this day and someday. No matter our age or spiritual maturity, our faith now isn't all that it could be or will be. Courage calls us to trust even in the quiet before the "Well?" can be spoken. At the same time, we live in expectation of what will come, even if a "Glory Hallelujah" cannot yet be fully conceived.

But as the days come, we'll need to know what we can count on. We'll need to know what to carry with us on the journey, because we have a choice to make, and it will matter what we decide. We stand at a proverbial fork in the road. This fork has three tines, three possible ways forward, each rich with possibilities. Each way will teach us something about God and about ourselves. Only one, however, takes us to our destination.

The first path has a signpost pointing the way. There's no mistaking what it says. It's well-lit and freshly painted. It says simply, "Sign." How odd. It's like sitting at a table that has the word *table* carved on its side. Except a sign is different. This isn't a self-label. A sign always points away from itself. So a sign of what? Where will this road take us?

~

It was a strange thing to be proud of, I admit. I was eleven, down on my knees, huddled under a school desk, my hands covering my head. I wasn't scared. It was an emergency drill at my elementary school, like the drills kids go through these days, but this one was designed to protect my classmates and me in case a missile with a nuclear warhead were to strike somewhere near us. Whether our little desks would have protected us from the nuclear blast or the radioactive fallout was never fully tested.

It wasn't the drill part that I was proud of. Those had become, sadly, routine. Rather, we knew that if World War III broke out, which seemed quite possible in those days, my town would be one of the first targets. Not New York City, not Los Angeles, but my town. Made my head swell with pride. It's not like I thought all of it through. I didn't want to die. I didn't even think about dying. It was just the feeling that I was part of something important.

Our town was near an airbase that was the home of the Strategic Air Command. The Soviets had targeted it for destruction if war broke out. So the US government commissioned twelve missile silos to be built around our town. They each housed an Atlas missile, the first operational intercontinental ballistic missile developed by the United States. The silos were 185 feet deep, with walls of concrete and epoxy-based resin built to withstand a nuclear blast. The missiles were designed to carry a nuclear payload to nearly any target in the Soviet Union. It was mad, literally MAD—mutually assured destruction—a show of force designed to prevent any of it from happening in the first place.

Most of the time we didn't worry about nuclear wars. We were kids, concerned about kids' things. But in October of 1962, we all had to worry about it. An American U-2 spy plane had captured photographic evidence of Soviet-built long-range missiles in Cuba. We were on the edge of an all-out war.

The B-52 Stratofortresses stationed at our Air Force base were taking off at all hours of the day and night. These were enormous bombers with eight roaring turbojet engines. If one of them were to be set on a football field, the wingspan would extend from the goal line to the opposing team's forty. During the crisis, at least fifty-six B-52s carrying nuclear weapons were in the air at all times. In addition to my town's—well, technically the country's—bombers and missiles, Navy ships blockaded Cuba. It was a massive demonstration of power combined with verbal sparring and secret diplomacy. The de-escalation of the crisis began in a matter of days.

Shows of force are what nations do. They're part of an arsenal of persuasion—aircraft carriers in the Persian Gulf, tests of nuclear warheads, economic sanctions, oil embargos, punitive tariffs, diplomats expelled, speeches delivered, tables pounded with a shoe. They're intended to intimidate, perhaps frighten, sometimes nudge, always to impress. Displays of power take different forms in different contexts. They're not just for nations but, at different levels of strength and seriousness, they are a part of any entity where people are involved, from businesses and schools to the Girl Scouts and the soccer team. And to churches, of course. Power is always at play in churches. All kinds of churches in all kinds of ways.

I've seen power wielded in churches based on the sheer number of members who are upset. I've seen power wielded by threats of lawsuits, social media campaigns, torrid gossip, displays of anger, and rivulets of tears. I've also seen power wielded through bold sermons, sensitive pastoral care, wise decision-making, and Christians on their knees in prayer.

Power is inevitable. It's always at play, not just in general but in each person's life of faith. Like what kind of God have we placed our trust in? And what role do we believe God plays concerning the things we need or desire? In and of itself, power is neither bad nor good. There are many kinds of power and many objects of power's effect. Control over another person in order to get one's way is one kind of power. Wisdom toward righteous ends is another. Gaslighting and deception are powers, as are kindness, charisma, prestige, and trustworthiness. Sometimes shows of power can help prevent a war. Sometimes power can destroy lives and nations. And churches.

The question is not how can we get rid of power but, rather, what or whom does power serve? Because power, despite its appearances, is not self-sufficient. Power is always in service to something or someone.

~

There was a power game going on among Christians in the ancient city of Corinth, though it might not have been easy to tell at first glance. The Christian community there was not one big church, with the choir and the band and all the big programs. It was scattered around the city in smaller gatherings of households and Christian neighbors. But not just scattered. They were also fractured—this group over and against that group, these needs running up against those. There were a lot of problems, a lot of conflicts. Some of the differences were about their loyalties—this house church identified with Paul, and that one was full of disciples of the great preacher Apollos, and the one over there idolized Simon. One of the house churches took great pride in just following Jesus.[1]

But some of the issues cut across all the groups. There were Christians suing other Christians in courts of law, sullying the name of Jesus in the city. Some were protecting and excusing a man having an affair with his stepmother. A bunch of them were arguing about whether it was okay to eat meat that had earlier been offered by pagan priests in sacrifice to their gods. And when all the house churches came together, all kinds of arguments broke out—about the Lord's Supper, about the wealthy and the poor, about the use of spiritual gifts, about who was the most important. What a mess. As most churches are.

So Paul wrote them a letter, the one we call 1 Corinthians, to address their conflicts and concerns. Not just to get at the surface-level stuff but to respond to the underlying causes. Here's where their problem with power shows up, in their understanding of God and their view of one another. Almost at the beginning of the letter, Paul says, "Jews ask for signs,"[2] a statement of both fact and critique. To be clear, it's not their Jewishness that's in question. Paul's concern is not their ethnicity but their ethics, their understanding of how God works in the world and, therefore, how Christians should.

When the ancient communities of faith talked about signs, they were generally referring to a miracle, some public display of supernatural power. But they also meant something more. On one occasion, the Pharisees pressed Jesus to give them a sign from heaven to prove that he had the authority from God to say the things he was saying.[3] He refused. Later in his ministry, Jesus talked about a day to come when the temple in Jerusalem would be destroyed. The people asked him, so what is the sign that this is about to take place?[4] A sign, then, was not just a miracle but a demonstration of power that confirmed someone's authority or that validated their message.

In the case of the Corinthian Christians, they wanted not just a miracle but something that showed how powerful they were and how much God was blessing them. They also believed the citizens of Corinth needed to observe the signs, like if we can't demonstrate our faith with powerful signs, then how will people know we're legit? How can we show that we're authentic, that we're right, that God is on our side? Without the show, why would the unbelievers believe?

Some of the Christians in Corinth had come to the three-tined fork in the road and had selected the first one. It was a way marked by power, by miraculous signs as proofs of God's approval of them. If, say, I can speak in tongues, then what does that say about me? What does God's choosing of me in this special way say about God? What does it say about the ones God has not blessed in the way God has blessed me? What if others have a gift, some sign from God, that I do not have? Could that mean God is validating their ministry more than mine? Isn't my gift special? My sign from God is more impressive, more important than those other gifts, right? If a special relationship with God validates me, shouldn't I desire that?

I remember well, and sometimes with embarrassment, my early years of ministry. In my late twenties and early thirties, I felt like the whole world was in front of me, that God had given me important work to do and had given me the tools to do that work. I had felt that as long as I could remember. The denomination I grew up in didn't use the language of ministerial calling. But even though I didn't know the word or its theological context, I felt it. I felt called from a very young age.

The preacher at my childhood church announced one Sunday morning that he would like to visit after the worship service with all the young people who desired to preach. I was ten years old at the time. I never hesitated. I told my parents I needed to be in that meeting and made my way back to the room. When I walked in, I realized my mistake. This was a campus church in a college town. The room was filled with college students. I was out of place. Way out of place. The preacher spotted me, rushed over, got down on his knees, and put his hands on my shoulders. I told him I wanted to be a preacher someday. I don't remember exactly what he said. I do remember his long hug and words of encouragement.

I have shared that story many times in my life. I don't remember using the word *sign* before, but that encounter when I was ten certainly felt like a sign from God, a validation from God about God's gifting, God's calling. Two decades later, I still felt that call. But I had chosen to do extensive graduate work rather than going straight into full-time ministry, so while I was doing coursework and serving as a part-time campus minister, many of my friends were in very public ministries serving at prestigious churches. It was hard. Better said, I felt sorry for myself. I kept wondering when it would be my time. I feel mortified just writing those words. I don't think I've ever told anyone those feelings. To do so, I would have to admit I was jealous, and jealousy is so unbecoming. And damaging. Not to mention sinful.

Around that time, I was invited to teach a class at a church conference. Not a keynote address like some of my friends, just a single class. Maybe this was the opportunity I was looking for. Surely God opened this door. I prepared for weeks. It was going to be really good. I was sure of it.

Three people came. Three. Afterwards, I filled a trash can with my unused class handouts. I was heartbroken. I kept thinking, hadn't God called me? Hadn't God gifted me? Hadn't I been shown that God wanted me to do ministry? Me. My gifts. My ministry. It was about me. About God's choosing me in some special way. What if others have a gift, some sign from God, that I do not have? Could that mean God is validating their ministry more than mine? Isn't my gift important? And so, I started digging missile silos deep inside. Not for offensive weapons. I didn't want to bring anyone down. I just wanted something to protect my heart.

My heart. But the purpose of signs is to point away from themselves. Signs point to something else, something other. That's their nature. Signs are good but only when they're making their point. Some signs simply aren't very good. They point badly—at the wrong things or in the wrong direction. Signs sometimes keep us from engaging the very thing they're pointing to. In other words, they miss the point. But often, the problem is us. The Corinthians were missing the point, even though the signs they sought were perfectly appropriate. I had missed the point. Until I figured that out, I would be useless in ministry.

~

Tucked away in the crevices of the Gospel of John, between two very public miracles, sits an innocuous little sentence. Just a transition. It's nothing, really. "A large crowd kept following [Jesus] because they saw the signs that he was doing for the sick."[5] I mean, that sentence doesn't really go anywhere. The very next sentence is about Jesus going up to the mountain to be with the Twelve. So, essentially, a large crowd had been following Jesus. They had witnessed or had at least heard about the signs Jesus had been performing, so they stayed around, but then he left them to go hang out with his buddies. And there the sentence sits. I suppose it's not that baffling. Amazing things were going on, and people wanted to see. But is that what the signs were for?

Signs in John focused on who Jesus was. There are seven signs in this Gospel. They all point away from themselves, all toward something important about Jesus. Jesus was God among us. The Word had become flesh. To know Jesus was to know the Father. So, how would the people know what God was like? How would they know what God was up to? Look for the signs.

The first sign was turning water into wine at a wedding feast in Cana (John 2). The second was the healing of the royal official's son in Capernaum (John 4). In that story, Jesus says, "Unless you see signs and wonders, you won't believe."[6] Don't miss the "you" here. The two occurrences of "you" in this sentence are plural—"y'all," as we say in Texas. So he's speaking not just to the royal official but also to the crowds. Unless y'all see signs, y'all won't believe. Is he suggesting that this is a good thing? Like, hallelujah, these signs are opening the door for y'all to believe in me. Or is it a problem? Y'all don't seem to believe in me unless you see some sort of sign. Which way did Jesus mean it? Let's let that one simmer for a bit. We'll get back to it.

The third sign was the healing of the man at the pool of Bethsaida on the Sabbath (John 5). After that, large crowds followed Jesus. They saw the signs. They wanted to see more. They kept following him. Word spread. The crowds became larger. Jesus taught them, but they were hungry. From a little bit of bread and fish, the disciples fed all five thousand of them (John 6). Sign number four. Then, "when the people saw the sign that he had done, they began to say, 'This is indeed the prophet who is to come into the world.'"[7]

This is great. The signs were doing their work. Look at those signs go. The signs pointed to God's anointed and to God's work. They were making things clear. Things are looking up. Faith was on the rise. The people were starting to get it. Then immediately, because of the sign Jesus had done—feeding all those hungry people—the crowds decided "to come and take [Jesus] by force to make him king."[8] Well, so much for the getting-it part.

After that little coronation attempt, Jesus, not surprisingly, withdrew from the crowds, walking across the lake on foot, its own little sign for the disciples in the boat. Sign number five, if you're still counting. (Signs six and seven come in John 9 and 11—the healing of the blind man in Jerusalem and raising his friend Lazarus from the dead.) But the crowds figured out where Jesus had gone and made their way to the other side of the lake to be with him. Jesus confronted them there. "The only reason you're looking for me," he said, and I paraphrase, "is because your bellies are full from the bread I gave you. You've missed the point. My signs are a window into God's heart, but you're not seeing it. You're just coming for the show. I'm not going to give you a show."[9]

Maybe we're getting closer to it now. We're looking for God. We want to be with God. We come together to praise God, to serve God. We want to show people God. Those things please God, surely. But the question is, why? What are we seeking? Why are we serving? What are we doing? What are we looking for? What are we showing? What's the point?

Or maybe the question is, what or whom am I pointing people to? "Look at everything our church is doing. We've got the best youth ministry. Look at those kids. Your kids oughta come sometime. They would enjoy doing things with our kids. Love our preacher. So funny. Preaches in jeans, shirttail out. Really cool. And the music. Moving, touching. I'm often brought to tears. And we've got all these great ministries. Doing good work. Helping folks. You oughta come join us." Common words of welcome for many church members. I love the spirit. But what are the words signaling? What's the story about? There are some markers, some signposts, but what's the destination the signposts are pointing to? The bottom line seems to be, we're doing great, we're good people, you would enjoy us, so come join in. Jesus said, "I tell you, you are looking for me not because you saw signs but because you ate your fill of the loaves."[10] If what you're seeking is the show, Jesus seems to be saying, I'm not planning to be there.

The signs should point to Jesus—to his mission, his relationship with his Father, to his love, his power, his ministry among us. You saw the signs, and they should have meant something to you. They should have called you closer to God. But you thought of yourselves first: "I was hungry, Lord, and you filled me up with miraculous loaves of bread. Not just me but thousands of us. From nothing. Wow. Super show. Now, do it again."

~

There are signposts along the road. We're glad to have them. They're important. They may not show up often, but when they do, our confidence that we're going in the right direction grows. The first signposts we saw, early on, were especially exciting. We knew then that we were on track, and we were grateful. But now, well along on the journey, if I constantly point to the signs, they lose their significance. "Look. Look at what I found. It's another SIGN! Look, everyone. Look at what I can do." The power of the sign is lost, what with all that attention on me.

Here's the point. It's easy, when you see a sign, to slip yourself into the picture. Some of the Christians in ancient Corinth were enamored with signs. But they couldn't just point to them; they had to take a selfie. In the church, two groups of sign followers were really going after it. Some were prophets. Their gift was not telling the future but telling the truth, speaking for God. Others were tongue speakers whose gifts were quite dramatic, but not everyone understood what they were talking about when they spoke in tongues. Both groups were reveling in their gifts, the miracles they could accomplish, the power they wielded. And they often wielded it against each other.

Paul takes sides on this matter: Of these two gifts, the gift of prophecy is better because people can understand it, Paul said.[11] Believers can understand. Outsiders can understand. But if someone speaks in a tongue and there's no one to translate what it means, it can be confusing. You've forgotten what the signs are for. They're not about you. Since you are striving after spiritual gifts, Paul says—if you're focusing your time and energy on having these powerful spiritual gifts—then at least do it in a way that builds up the church.[12] Use the signs to serve others. They're not to display your power or build up your reputation.

The signpost is a road marker. The fact that you've spotted it doesn't mean your faith is stronger than anyone else's. See the sign. Be thankful. But don't forget what a sign is for. It points to God. Always. And it blesses those around you. That point is clear a few verses earlier, in the most well-known of all the passages in this letter.

"Strive for the greater gifts," Paul says at the end of 1 Corinthians 12—in other words, some gifts are more helpful than others—"and I will show you a still more excellent way." Then he gets into the heart of the matter: "If I speak in the tongues of humans and of angels but do not have love, I am a noisy gong or a clanging cymbal. And if I have prophetic powers . . . but do not have love, I am nothing."[13] Love is patient and kind and isn't envious or boastful and doesn't insist on its own way. Like Jesus. Look for the signs. They all point to him.

And the gifts God gives us? Well, they're for other people. They reflect God, but their purpose is to serve others. Make sure the attention goes where it belongs. It doesn't matter whether they know what you've done, whether they're impressed. And if you feel called by God for some task or ministry, your calling is not about you either. Your calling doesn't belong to you. It's not for you to control. It's not your job to compare it with others'. It's to serve and, in your service, to point to Jesus. And if you hear God or see God, great. Receive the encounter with joy. Treat it as a signpost and keep looking down the road. But if you make it about you, the sign loses its purpose and its power.

Okay. I have a confession to make. Confessions are not easy, at least not for me, but I think I need to come clean here. I sometimes find it difficult to hear someone say, "God told me." You may have picked up on that. I shouldn't think that way, but I sometimes do. But here's the honest truth. There's not a lot of difference between "God told me" and "God never tells me anything." They reflect the same problem. I sometimes doubt. But to wear it as a badge ends up making it about me—my insights, my need to be seen, my control, my power.

"Unless you see signs and wonders, you won't believe," Jesus said when he healed the son of the royal official. Unless you see the show, unless you're wowed and awed, you won't believe. And that's a problem. John isn't going to let us miss the point. Those words are almost verbatim what John records a few chapters later when the apostle Thomas said about the newly resurrected Jesus, "Unless I see the mark of the nails in his hands and put my finger in the mark of the nails and my hand in his side, I will not believe."[14] But after he touched Jesus's scars, after the wow and awe, Thomas believed. Then Jesus said to him, "Have you believed because you have seen me?" That's good, Thomas. Congratulations. Welcome to the kingdom. But here's the hard part: "Blessed are those who have not seen and yet have come to believe."[15]

Perhaps my spending more time in bed these last few weeks than I ever have in my life has allowed me to see some things I hadn't seen before. I haven't been able to get in to a cardiologist yet and don't know what's the matter with my heart. So maybe I've been able to focus on some things I've been avoiding. Here's where my mind has traveled.

I imagine myself at Jesus's side, right next to Thomas. "Lord," I say after mustering a little courage. "Lord, some of my friends tell me that God speaks to them, but God never seems to speak to me. I don't see God everywhere. I need to touch your wounds with my own hand. Can you give me the same show you gave Thomas? I want to see the signs and wonders too." Or maybe I need to say something a little more honest. "Lord, I don't hear God's voice, but I'm here anyway, which surely is a sign of my superb faith. I heard what you said to Thomas. I'm the guy you were telling him about. I haven't seen, and I still believe. That's the sign I was looking for. I am my own sign. I hope you're impressed, Lord."

I've sometimes been skeptical of those who need to see signs. But I fear I've been seeking signs too. I just do so by letting others know that God isn't showing me any. Or worse, that I am the hero of my own story, the doubting one who believes in God anyway. In that light, my story may be less about doubt than it is about control. Honest doubt pushes me to ask, seek, and knock. Doubt nudges my faith toward God. But making sure you know that I'm not like others isn't about faith. It's about me.

I've got some things to think about. I may need to crawl under a school desk for a little while, my hands covering my head, down on my knees.

07

WHEN IN TRUTH, TELL THE DOUBT

I found myself a step behind in too many of my conversations, and I wasn't happy about it. That's not exactly true. I was actually several steps behind, and I was terrified. I was in a new job in a new line of work in a new city. I hated to look like I didn't know what I was doing, but, in fact, I didn't know what I was doing.

I had been asked to lead a nonprofit organization, doing something I believed in—fighting for the neighbors in one of the poorest neighborhoods in the country. Our mission, in part, was to help transform low-income neighborhoods and to build a replicable model for urban revitalization. I was coming in with no experience in transforming neighborhoods and no knowledge about urban revitalization. But I believed in the cause and was all in. It meant, however, that I would need to work closely with folks who did things—important things that were crucial to the effectiveness of our work—about which I knew absolutely nothing.

I remember sitting in a meeting on the first day at my job. Around the table were an architect with a long history of neighborhood revitalization, a long-time community activist, and an expert in urban renewal, all folks who worked closely with the mayor, the city manager, the city council, as well as church and business leaders on issues of poverty in the city. I, on the other hand, had been a minister and a teacher, jobs that proved in this moment to be of no use whatsoever.

The founder of our organization, who was an influential figure in the city, introduced me to the group gathered around the table as "our new president and CEO." That was the high point of the meeting for me. The discussion went immediately into high gear, and things fell apart for me fast. We were working to get funding for the neighborhood through the CDE for projects that benefited both LICs and LMIs. The DDF, which, of course, is part of the CDE, administers NMTC benefits from the US Department of the Treasury to distressed communities. The important thing, though, was getting a CDBG grant.

My mind began to turn into goopy mush. I pulled my phone out as inconspicuously as I could and googled "CDE." It stood for Community Development Entity. Yes, I thought. Good. Now I'm getting somewhere. Except, wait. I have no idea what that means. Keep reading. So, a Community Development Entity is "a domestic corporation or partnership that is an intermediary vehicle for the provision of loans, investments, or financial counseling in low-income communities." Ah, so low-income communities must be what an LIC is. Bingo. But what is an "intermediary vehicle"? I once owned an intermediary vehicle in graduate school—an old car I had for a few months until I could pick up the one I was buying from a friend—but I was pretty sure that was not what was being discussed here. I was lost.

The conversation kept moving forward at high speed. I got further behind. No way my thumb-Googling could keep up. I heard my name, but it didn't quite register. They couldn't be asking me a question. I'm the new guy. But there it was again. The chair of the meeting was looking at me. "Jack," he said for at least the third time, "what do you think? Should we put an RFP together or just an RFI?" I pondered this question for a moment like a chess master contemplating several moves ahead—let's see, if my bishop takes his knight, it will cost me the bishop, but I will still be a knight up, which can take his rook, which would leave his queen undefended . . . "Well," I said, looking as thoughtful as my current terrified state would allow, "I'm wondering if it might be too early for an RFP."

I had no idea what I was talking about. I was just playing off his sentence. Obviously, an RFI was somehow less definitive or less demanding than an RFP. That's all I could come up with for my one contribution to the meeting. "Yes," he said. "I think you're right. Okay, let's hold off on the RFP for the time being. Jack, could you get a preliminary RFI to us by the end of the day?"

Sure. Sure I could. Be happy to. First, of course, I would have to find out what the hell an RFI was.

Knowledge matters. Knowledge is important. Knowledge is power. Knowledge lifts you up. Knowledge is an enticing path forward, the second tine of our fork at the crossroads we have come to. What could possibly be wrong with wanting more knowledge?

All my life I have worked to make sure I knew what I needed to know, not just to know much but to know well, not more than anyone else but enough to be good at my work. But knowledge can also let you down. It can be insufficient for the task at hand. Not all knowledge is useful. Or said differently, knowledge that's useful in one context may not be relevant in another. I could explain to my urban renewal team the origins and implications of the Documentary Hypothesis in the composition of the Pentateuch and could wax eloquently on the Synoptic problem in the Gospels, but none of that information would help get loan money to businesses in blighted neighborhoods or put food on the table for our neighbors who had no table to eat at or home to live in.

There's a line in Paul's first letter to the Corinthian Christians that comes to mind. I flinch a little when I read it: "Knowledge puffs up."[1] Yeah. Yeah, it does. I had placed a lot of stock in knowledge throughout my life. All work requires it—plumbers have to know how to plumb, insurers how to insure, teachers how to teach. You have to know things in order to do things. Knowledge can empower you. It can make you a better citizen, a better Christian, a better person. But it can also make you arrogant, above it all, above others.

Let's put this stake in the ground: Knowledge has limits. Period. Knowledge on any subject, knowledge about one's own life, knowledge about God, about God's ways, about what God may or may not be doing. Recognition of the limitations of knowledge doesn't mean that individuals shouldn't know as much as they can. There is no such thing as having too much knowledge. The issue isn't quantity. The issue, rather, is what knowledge can do to a person—the way we can come to think about ourselves or compare ourselves or celebrate ourselves because of whatever knowledge we may have gained in life.

One of the aims of a good education is recognizing the limits of what we know. Younger students generally aren't yet aware of their limits and haven't yet gained appropriate filters. Scientists have proven—I'm fairly certain about this—that the pinnacle of human knowledge comes in a person's life at around the age of nineteen. Late teenagers generally know more about the world than their parents, their teachers, or any genius who has ever lived. In my experience, few students speak to their teachers with as much confidence as sophomores in college, whether they know what they're talking about or not. They know just enough to know that they know some things, but they don't yet know enough to know what they don't know. Or that they don't know. After this high point of human understanding, education is about teaching us how little we actually know.

The more knowledgeable we are, whether through schooling or by life, the less we know. That is, the less we know for sure. The more we learn, the more questions we should have. That's what doubt is for. That's why doubt is beneficial. In science, every assumption, every hypothesis, every conclusion must be doubted. Doubt is a crucial part of the modern scientific method. Questioning the results of our research is how knowledge is advanced, which should be true not just in science but also in faith and in life. Doubt, in this case, is not directed at God but at ourselves. Having healthy doubt about ourselves means that what we think we know will be tamed by humility.

Social scientists have found substantial evidence for what is called the Dunning-Kruger effect, named after the psychologists who first described it: People overestimate what they know. Specifically, people who know a lot in one area often assume that they know a lot in other areas. It's a common human characteristic that we often misjudge what we know. Or, as the younger President Bush used to say, we "misunderestimate" the problem. When that happens, a lesson in humility can result. Or, worst-case scenario, humiliation.

It happened to me a few days ago. I was at a social gathering. There were a lot of people in the room. It was noisy. I'm a little hard of hearing. Okay, sorry, those are pre-excuses for what happened. Lesa's business partner and a mutual acquaintance were sharing stories about the American Midwest. It was just small talk. Nothing at stake. There was no reason for me to impose myself on their conversation. But I misunderestimated the situation, and I misoverestimated my competence.

The two women had grown up in the Midwest. They were sharing things that were different up north than they are down in Texas, about things they missed, especially certain foods. They waxed on and on about the dumplings that are common in much of the Midwest, made of dough wrapped around a filling—cheese, potatoes, pork, fruit, almost anything—and boiled, then fried. They're called pierogies. The women referred to these delicious dumplings by name, but I was perhaps not as focused on the conversation as I should have been. I was tired and may have been limited in the attention I needed to stay in the conversation. But not, apparently, limited in self-assurance.

No worries. I'm good at small talk. I knew exactly what they were referring to. After all, I lived in the Midwest for four years, so I was knowledgeable about Midwestern things and was more than happy to share what I knew. "Oh yes," I broke in confidently. "I love those Peyronies. Had them all the time when I lived up north. Savory Peyronies. Sweet Peyronies. You know, Peyronies are a lot like empanadas," I told them. They looked at me, I don't know, strangely. Peyronie's, as you may know if you watch television commercials, is something else altogether, a physical condition nothing like boiled dumplings. I had inadvertently thrown a curve into the conversation. I blushed and apologized.

You don't know much of anything until you discover how little you actually know, until someone challenges you, until you can say "I don't know" or "I was wrong." Or "Sorry about the Peyronie's thing." But discernment about our limited knowledge seems rare these days.

~

We live in a time when what we think we know is funneled through media that is increasingly narrow—national media, local media, social media, and our own networks of friends who think as we do. We each have our version of the facts—alternative facts we've been told, as if each side needs just the arguments that prop up our own positions—which are then fed by online algorithms that are self-reinforcing so that we can't imagine that anyone could arrive at conclusions different from our own. What's the matter with you people? The truth is plain as day. Just open your eyes. You want truth? I got your truth right here.

And I'm not talking simply about national politics, which is exasperating enough. Our limited personal universes of knowledge make it difficult to have meaningful conversations about faith and doubt or about the presence or absence of God in our lives. Our understanding of the working of God plays out on every side—for those who doubt a lot and those who never doubt at all. Both ends of that continuum can be guilty of the self-puffery that comes from too much confidence about what we know, or think we know.

On one side of the spectrum are believing Christians who are hesitant to rely on supernatural explanations for human experiences. They believe in God's involvement in our world but are not ready to claim that God speaks to humans directly. Surely, they say, God is not breaking the laws of science and nature to get inside our brains to tell us about the new job God thinks we ought to take over at the bank across town.

To understand these folks a little better, we'll need to dip our toes into the current conversations about "disenchantment," a discussion that intersects our concerns here about faith and doubt.[2] The conversation about disenchantment and the modern world dates to

1917, when the German sociologist Max Weber first used the word: "The fate of our times is characterized by rationalization and intellectualization and, above all, by the 'disenchantment of the world.'"[3] Weber's word in German literally means to "de-magic-ize." Our modern world has become un-magicked or disenchanted.

There was a time when everyone, and I mean everyone, assumed not only the existence of a spirit world but that this spirit world collided with our physical world everywhere, all the time. Virtually everything could be explained through supernatural causes—health and disease, crop success or failure, the weather, business prospects, marital happiness, the birth of children, the succession of kings, victory or defeat in battle, everything. If a child died or a building collapsed or a ship ran aground or a monarch lived an especially long life, the cause could be traced to some spiritual reality: The gods were fighting or were pleased with us or were manipulating us humans; or God was angry or capricious or had a mysterious plan for this person or that.

In this enchanted world, magic was assumed to be real. Witchcraft was real. Alchemy was real. The trees and skies, animals and birds, rivers and storms were brimming with spiritual energy. From the perspective of, well, anyone who lived prior to the last couple hundred years or so, spirit and flesh crossed over on a regular basis. What we might call superstition they would have called the working of God in the world. Or it could be the spirit of darkness. This spirit-filled universe was inescapable. It was the world they all knew to be true.

One example: A thousand years ago, when Christians gathered in churches, the highlight of the service was not the sermon and not the taking of communion, which few of them did anyway. If the bread at the communion table became the actual body of Jesus, which they all believed, then most of them felt unworthy to eat Christ's body. Their holy moment, rather, came when the priest uttered the Prayer of Consecration, when the bread was blessed. That was the moment the bread was transformed into the body of Jesus.

The priest did the deed by citing Jesus's words at the Last Supper, "This is my body." Except, of course, the priest said it in Latin, "*Hoc est corpus meum."* That's what the worshippers heard at the moment of the miracle: "*Hoc est corpus meum.*" Say it fast three times and you'll hear it. The worshippers, who couldn't understand Latin, heard the words as "hocus pocus," which is why that phrase eventually became associated not with the Eucharist but with magic. People believed diseases could be cured as well as other miracles merely by viewing the newly blessed bread. What seems like superstition to us was a regular part of their spiritual existence. The world was enchanted. To be clear, the problem wasn't the nature of the sacrament itself. Rather, at least from a modern perspective, it was ascribing to the ritual of the Lord's Supper the powers of magic.

But over the last few hundred years, the world has been demystified. Science—biology, agriculture, genetics, physics, astronomy, medicine, economics, psychology, and on and on—can describe how natural phenomena work without resorting to supernatural explanations. In our day, the formerly enchanted world has become disenchanted.

So, what do you do as a person of faith, when you believe in God's active presence in the world but also the scientific explanations of the universe? Can the world be disenchanted and, at the same time, full of the glory of God? Said differently, can the world be God-enchanted, God-inhabited, and God-touched while still adhering to all the physical laws of the universe? Can we believe in both science and miracles? Can we have faith in a living God while believing that God's hand is not always detectable, traceable, or tangible? Can you have faith in God's active presence among us and also have doubts? This is the tension many Christians feel. It can be a tough balance.

On the opposite side of the spectrum are those who have no trouble at all believing in an enchanted world. The world is alive with the presence of God. Miracles happen all the time. My friends who live comfortably in such a world nevertheless live every day as modern people in a modern world. They're not anti-science. They believe in and respect the laws of science and nature. They know the difference between magic and reality. But they are far more open to the idea that

God engages human lives here and now in profound and substantial ways, that God performs miracles still, and that those miracles are visible, knowable, and real.

They are not just comfortable with the notion of a God-enchanted world; they rely on it. It's a crucial part of their faith. People have cancer and God cures them. Not every time, but when it happens, it's a cause for praise and rejoicing. A life situation has become especially difficult, and God pulls them out of it and into a place where they can thrive. Some may hear God say something audible to them. Others discern God's voice differently. This, too, is authentic, faithful Christian living.

Whatever we may believe, all our knowledge about the working of God in our midst is reinforced by the people we know, the books we read, our everyday experiences, our lived realities. Those realities, however, are largely isolated from one another. There's little overlap, little dialogue, and little openness to see things differently. We know what we know, and we are shaped by what we believe. Reinforced by our friends and experiences, we become confident in our own knowledge. That confidence in what we think we know is often the source of the problem.

There's a sentence in Paul's Letter to the Romans that I had not seen until a few years ago. I don't know how I could have missed it, really. In fact, Paul says it twice, and just a few sentences apart. It's almost as if he thought this idea was really important to his readers, like if they had known this truth and practiced it, the church in Rome wouldn't have so many problems: "Do not claim to be wiser than you are."[4]

Just a few paragraphs earlier, Paul makes a complicated argument about how gentiles have been grafted into the Jewish tree and how Israel will be saved. The fact that scholars have disagreed for centuries and disagree today about Paul's meaning here underscores his very point: "I want you to understand this mystery, brothers and sisters, so that you may not claim to be wiser than you are."[5]

There are a lot of things you don't know, Paul says. You may not be as smart as you think. Knowledge is a good thing, but knowing you don't know everything ought to make you humble. So be careful when you make your claims about what God is or is not doing, what God can or cannot do, what you understand or think you understand about God. Don't claim to be wiser than you are. Keep your doubts about your own knowledge and abilities close at hand. They serve an important purpose. They may keep you from making a fool of yourself. Mark Twain famously said, "When in doubt, tell the truth." The greater lesson may be, "When in truth, tell the doubt."

When Hurricane Katrina tore up the city of New Orleans in 2005, I heard lots of stories about what God was doing in this storm, spoken with utter confidence. The basic message was that Hurricane Katrina was not a random weather event. God sent it, and God sent it for a very good reason.

One prominent Christian evangelist said that God sent this devastating hurricane because of the sinfulness of New Orleans. "This is one wicked city," he said. "It's known for Mardi Gras, for Satan worship. It's known for sex perversion. It's known for every type of drugs and alcohol and the orgies and all of these things that go on down there in New Orleans. . . . God is going to use that storm to bring revival."[6]

Except that the French Quarter, the focus of this preacher's wrath, received less damage from Katrina than any other part of the city. That part of New Orleans is on higher ground, so the flooding from Katrina wasn't as devastating there. The greatest damage was done in St. Bernard Parish and the Ninth Ward, the lowest and poorest sections of town. The poverty of these neighborhoods had grown directly from the city's practice of redlining a few decades earlier when white city leaders, for generations, prevented Black families from moving into white neighborhoods. The ones hurt the most by the hurricane were the most vulnerable, the most victimized, the most innocent. Why would God have done that? And why would anyone think that the sin of the French Quarter was more despicable to God than the sins of these white city leaders a few decades earlier?

But other observers had other ideas about this storm. The head of a major Christian nonprofit said God sent Katrina to wake us up to possible terrorist attacks. The president of a prominent Christian university linked Katrina to the confirmation hearings of Supreme Court nominee John Roberts as a warning to Roberts and the senators about America's abortion policies and practices. A well-known Christian author argued that Katrina occurred as proof that God's judgment of America had begun.[7]

These claims about the reasoning and working of God can't all be true, of course. Each was based on the notion that God sent this hurricane or at least controlled the path of the storm, choosing where it would land, what damage it would cause, and who would be injured or killed. The cumulative effect of these confident and contradictory judgments, all in the name of God, has consequences. At the very least, they can make God look petty and the Christian faith foolish.

At the same time, those of us who are perhaps more skeptical about claims that the spiritual realm has broken into our physical world can reveal the same sort of hubris in our own lives. When someone says, "God told me" or "God sent a hurricane," we may think to ourselves: That wasn't God. It couldn't have been. It's more likely your imagination or the self-fulfillment of your own desires. God simply doesn't do that.

Perhaps. It's interesting, though, that a major tenet of the scientific method, which has played such a significant role in the disenchantment of our world, states that in any research, one cannot prove the null hypothesis. In other words, you can't prove nonexistence. As most statistics teachers will say at some point, "Absence of evidence is not evidence of absence." In other words, it's hard to prove the existence of a non-action, that something did not happen. Proving that God did not do something is impossible. Be careful about the claims you make, especially about what you think others did or did not experience from God.

Let's set our certainty aside for a moment. Some things can't be known for sure. Don't claim to be wiser than you are. The axiom "Knowledge puffs up" is true both for those who doubt and for those who are certain. This is the problem with knowledge, the downside of those times when we think we know what God has or has not done. We overlook God's hiddenness. Hiddenness is in God's nature. Claiming that we know what we cannot know is in ours.

Humans have always sought to know more than we can know. It's the story of the first humans in the garden. It's the story of the building of the great tower. It's Moses asking to see God's face, God's glory. The Preacher of Ecclesiastes summed up the wisdom he had gained in his life with these words: "I saw all the work of God, that no one can find out what is happening under the sun. However much they may toil in seeking, they will not find it out; even though those who are wise claim to know, they cannot find it out."[8] However much we may want to know, there are some things we cannot know. God's ways are hidden.

The problem with the way of knowledge, however, is more than its tendency toward hubris, of claiming we know more than we know. It's the belief that knowledge itself will provide the answers we need: We can solve things, create things, fix things if only we had more data, if we just knew more. The stunning recent developments in artificial intelligence are challenging that notion. There is no possible way that humans can "know" what ChatGPT or other AI programs can know. AI systems have access to the massive digitally stored archives of human knowledge and can spit back answers to profoundly difficult questions in seconds. The amalgamation of knowledge bits will continue to increase, but that doesn't mean we know more.

One of the limitations of human knowledge is the assumption that knowledge itself can provide the answers we need. To be human, as Princeton historian of science and technology D. Graham Burnett has said, "is not to have answers. It is to have *questions*—and to live with them. The machines can't do that for us. Not now, not ever."[9] The heart of our humanity resides not in the sum total of our knowledge but in the questions we ask.

While technological advances can simulate what it means to know and expand that knowledge far beyond what any human could possibly know, the machines cannot know what it means to be human. The *doing* part of power and the *knowing* part of knowledge can never re-create the human part—which is also to say the divine part, the God-given part—of *being*. Humans, because we are created in God's image, can do what knowledge-centered systems cannot. We can live, we can care, we can wait, we can sin, we can hurt, we can hope, we can surrender.

~

Both the way of signs and the way of knowledge are limited. They rely on human abilities. They seek God straight ahead. But most of the time, God can be glimpsed over to the side, humbly, unexpectedly. Like in an executioner's bloody field, where the glory of God was in full display as a small crowd gathered around a dying man who was singing a song about God's absence. Or two days later, as two friends walked together on a seven-mile journey from Jerusalem to a little nothing village. They were telling a perfect stranger that they had just witnessed the death of Jesus, not knowing it was actually Jesus, the risen Christ, they were talking to. They were face-to-face with the Son of God and did not see him. On the other hand, they weren't expecting to see him. He had died on Friday.

They had been with Jesus before. They knew him. They loved him. As they walked, their hearts burned within them. But they didn't see him. They invited the stranger to join them for dinner. Jesus sat down and ate with them, and they still didn't know. Until he blessed the bread. Then their eyes were opened. Then they knew. Only for Jesus to vanish from their midst. They were with him, then he was gone. Hidden again. But they raced back to Jerusalem to the place where the disciples had gathered. They told them what had happened, about how they didn't recognize Jesus and then how they did when he broke bread with them.[10]

What kind of God is this whose presence is hidden, whose face we don't recognize in a conversation along the road but rather in a common act performed at meals? And what kind of faith would nudge us to run seven miles back up the road we had just come from to tell others that we had seen the Son of God? Where would such a faith come from? What would such a faith look like?

Some of the Christians in ancient Corinth, as we have seen, were pursuing the signs thing. They had fallen in love with signs. Big displays of divine power. They wanted God to show up with strength, with miracles. Surely, that's how the unbelievers would know who Jesus was. Besides, those who could wield the power of the signs would get a lot of attention. They had taken the first road.

But there was an alternative, a second way. "Jews ask for signs," Paul said, "and Greeks desire wisdom." In other words, you can see God through much learning, through knowledge, through wisdom. This way of wisdom was enticing. Especially here. Especially in Corinth. Because Corinth was a city full of wise teachers.

Corinth was witnessing a renaissance of wisdom. Wise teachers were in abundance. Each teacher had disciples who paid good money for what they were learning. These wise men were impressive. They taught rhetoric to their disciples and were themselves known as great public speakers. Better than Paul. At least that's what Paul thought.[11] They were good. Very good. If the gospel is going to have an impact here in Corinth, then we will have to be smarter than that. We will have to be better, more impressive.

So what about us? What sort of strategy should we use? We want to change the world. For God's sake, the world needs changing. What can the power people do? What role can the knowledge people play? It's going to be tough. At least two obstacles stand in the way: How can we count on God if God continues to hide, and what can humans do if we keep screwing things up?

08

WE'RE ALL BROKEN, BUT SOME AIN'T BROKE YET

We were on the road to see Lesa's dad. He's ninety-three and living strong as of this writing. He broke his hip a few months ago but is already galloping around the assisted living center with his walker, joking with the nurses, telling stories to the other residents in the dining room or to guests in the lobby. We were on our way to check in on him, listening to an audiobook as we often do on the road.

Our favorite books lately have been biographies and autobiographies, which we find not only interesting but often inspiring. This time it was Brandi Carlile's memoir. Brandi says something near the beginning of chapter six that neither of us had ever heard before. We hit the thirty-second rewind and played it again. My brain was churning. I had to think about this. It was her own story, but what she said seemed to point to a larger truth.

If you don't know Brandi Carlile, she performs Americana music, among other genres. Americana sits in the gap between several musical styles—folk, bluegrass, country, gospel, rock, blues, indie, pop, and I'm sure others. Her music is hard to categorize, except to say that it's passionate, personal, authentic, and moving.

There was a time during a particularly dark season of my life when Brandi's music—her voice, her harmonies, and her lyrics—sustained me. I almost said saved me. That would only be a slight exaggeration.

I can't remember when I first knew of her. Somewhere in the early 2000s. For a couple of decades or so, I had largely set my music aside. Music is not my profession, but it is a passion, the fuel for my creative self. For a while—a fairly long while—I stopped, or mostly stopped, playing my piano or guitar. I hardly listened to music in any form. I don't remember all the reasons why. I was busy with graduate school, and then full-time ministry, then teaching. Lots of life going on. Some very good things. A few difficult things. I was happy much of the time and mostly fulfilled. I didn't see the depression coming.

After the years of disengagement, I felt a deep urge to begin looking for some music and musicians that I had not listened to before. In other words, singers younger than me. I discovered musicians like Ray LaMontagne, Lucy Kaplansky, Dar Williams, and Amos Lee. Somewhere in there, Brandi's music slipped into my consciousness. I saw her, along with the Hanseroth twins and the rest of her band, in a small, intimate concert in Dallas, barely a hundred folks or so, much smaller than her normal gigs. It was unforgettable.

I didn't know her story at the time. But I left the concert knowing two things: Her music touched me deeply, and she was a person of faith. I hadn't read the faith part anywhere, and she didn't mention it in the concert. I could just tell. How is that possible? If there was some stranger out there who knew as little about me as I did of her, could they tell I had faith? I'm not sure. But with her, somehow I knew.

She published her memoir, *Broken Horses*, in 2021. It's a remarkable story told well. She talks about being a teenager in rural Washington, living with her family in a small trailer home. At one point in the story, she got a horse, a retired racehorse named Drummer. The horse was broken. It was here that Brandi made an important distinction, one I will never forget.

As you already know, I grew up in West Texas, in cowboy country, so I obviously already knew a lot about horses and cattle. The cowboys of Saskatchewan could confirm this fact, of course, but since they're scrupulously honest, they probably won't. Perhaps I should have known the contrast that Brandi made. You may already know.

Maybe everyone does. But I didn't know. Brandi distinguished between horses that were broken and horses that were broke. When Lesa and I heard it, our brains sort of exploded. We talked about it for a while. It was a critical clue in my changing understanding of faith and the presence of God. That was not her purpose. Whether it was God's, I don't know.

Drummer, she said, was a broken horse. He had a broken leg. He also was broke, but, as Brandi explains, that's a different thing altogether.

> To be "broke," a horse must allow a person to believe that it is afraid enough to be conquered, tamed, and ridden. It's never true. They don't break. I've never been thrown, kicked, or stepped on by a wild horse . . . they've always been "broke." Horse people never say a horse is broken. Even when it would seem to make sense. . . .
>
> "Can I ride him?"
>
> "No! He ain't broke yet."[1]

This distinction between broken and broke is important and not just for horses. A lot of people are broken. In fact, I would argue that all humans are. Some know it and some don't. Some admit it and some hide it, sometimes from themselves. Brokenness is in our nature. It's inescapable. It's how we were created. We don't live forever. Life breaks us down, one thing after another, reminding us of our mortality, hinting to us that there's something more.

We're all broken, but some ain't broke yet. Being broken is not the same as being broke. Broke is an act of our will. It requires surrender. It's a clear and decisive letting go, a new self-understanding that we are not in control but have been, in fact, conquered, that we belong to another, that we belong to God, that we were bought at a price more costly than we can get our minds around. Being broke requires trust. It is driven not by what we do but by what we relinquish, what we forgo, what we are free of.

To allow ourselves to be broke, we'll need to first come to grips with our brokenness. Being broken is a prerequisite to being broke. It's necessary, but it's not enough. It's hard to imagine how any of us could surrender control of our lives if we had never been broken before or hadn't come to realize how broken we already are.

Broken is something that happens to us, like falling, breaking a hip, and learning to walk again, with a limp and some pain, and sometimes a little joking with the nurses. Or we do it to ourselves by making bad decisions in which we bring pain or loss to our own body or soul as well as the people around us. But broke is different. It's a choice we make to give ourselves over to something else, to be tamed, to trust even when we don't know for sure. In relation to God, Christians have generally called a life choice of that sort, well, faith.

Being broken is a state of being. Being broke is a risk. Being broken may be more painful. Being broke will be more costly. With brokenness comes some sort of diminishment—health, career, reputation, finances, relationships, heart. With broke-ness comes promise and hope.

Allowing ourselves to be broke does a couple of things. Like the aperture in a pre-smartphone camera, surrendering to God lets the light in. We want to see God. We want to know God. We need proper light in order to focus, so that the imprint can be made. But we also need to know where to look, where to point the camera. The shot we're aiming for has too often been on ourselves. And so, our quest for glimpses of God in our selfie-oriented culture tends to be inward: What can I see? Where is God in my life? Where is God in relation to me? What is God doing for me? What is God showing me?

But when we are broke, not just life-broken but God-broke, the nature of our surrender will change our angle of vision. We will see God differently. Our orientation will shift. God will become visible in surprising places and in surprising ways. But the first thing we will have to do is give up control. It won't be easy. Being broke comes with a cost.

~

"Rabbi?" the young student asked as he approached the old teacher hesitantly.

This is the beginning of a story I've told for years. I heard it somewhere. I don't remember where. Nor do I know if it actually happened. I've done some research, but I can't find a definitive answer. It may be a story told by Rabbi Menachem Mendel Morgensztern, a beloved nineteenth-century Polish rabbi.

One of the rabbi's favorite maxims was, "There is nothing more whole than a broken heart." This quote hints at the meaning of the story I have been telling all these years. Whether or not it happened is inconsequential. Its truth lies in the telling of it, and the hearing.

"Rabbi?" the young student asked as he approached the old man. "I don't understand. You taught us today from Deuteronomy that God puts his word upon our hearts.[2] And from Proverbs, you told us that God's word was written on the tablet of our hearts."[3]

"Yes, my son," the rabbi replied. "You heard me well."

"But why," the young man asked, "does God put his word *upon* our hearts? Why does he not put his word *within* our hearts?"

The rabbi stroked his long beard. "My son, not even God can put his word within our hearts. He puts his word upon our hearts so that when our hearts break, the first thing that enters is the word of God."

~

Three friends were in Aswan, Egypt, one of the oldest and most important cities in the long history of Egypt. They were on this journey together because, one way or another, they were looking for something. What exactly they were looking for, I'm not sure they even knew. One of the men, my friend Daz, who was twenty-seven at the time, describes his story as "a long brokenness." Somehow his brokenness, his emptiness, had brought him to Aswan, where millennia ago the stones for the construction of the ancient pyramids were hewn from the nearby hills and cut into usable blocks.

Daz's given name is Darren, though few people in his life called him Darren, except sometimes his mother and a few friends. He's Australian, and people in Australia named Darren are often called Daz. At age fifteen, Daz had consciously rejected Christianity. He had grown up in a home where he was taught Scripture. His father was an Anglican minister. Daz went to an Anglican school where institutionally endorsed Christian teachings were everywhere. But he didn't love it.

In that year, Daz's father and mother separated. A few years earlier, Daz's aunt had been murdered, a family trauma that affected everyone in the family—his parents' deteriorating marriage and certainly Daz's own sense of brokenness. In the wake of these traumas, Daz turned his back on the church. He didn't think of it so much as turning his back on Jesus, but fifteen-year-old Daz didn't really make that distinction. He was simply done.

Looking back on it, Daz describes his next twelve years as walking in darkness. His mum prayed for him, continually and fervently, but she could see no sign of the change she was praying for. He pursued every pleasure you can imagine. He was in London, in the banking business, when he had an "Ecclesiastes moment." Even though he had tasted most everything that the world could offer him, he found it all very empty. And so, after a dozen years of not even thinking about Jesus or church, Daz and his two friends began a season of travel. Daz was hoping to find purpose and perspective. In June of 2004, they were in far southern Egypt, in Aswan. Their sleeping quarters were a boat on the Nile.

There, in his sleep, Daz had a dream. In the dream, he and his two friends were walking down the road. He was feeling a kind of ecstasy—not the drug-induced sort, though he knew what that was like, but a deep feeling of euphoria, an indescribable ecstasy, unlike anything he had ever experienced. In this dream, Jesus appeared and said to him, "I am the way, the truth, and the life."

Then the scene shifted to the day of judgment. Somehow in this judgment, Daz says, he was spared. He had no way of explaining that. Jesus asked him, "Why haven't you told your friends about Jesus before?" So, Daz turned to his friends—again, still in the dream—and asked them, "Do you believe Jesus died for your sins?" One of the friends he was traveling with—let's call him Jeff—replied: "No." So, he watched his friends being sentenced to judgment. In an attempt to comfort them, Daz told them, "Don't worry. Hell is just separation from God," but then he realized that his desire to comfort might not be all that comforting.

He woke up. It was about four in the morning. The three of them were going to leave for an excursion to a temple built by Ramses II. His friends were already awake. Before they left, Daz knew he had to say something. "I had a strange dream last night," he said. Jeff responded, "Yeah, I had a strange dream, too, about a mountain falling, and I knew how to get people out, but I didn't help them, and I felt sort of guilty about it. What was your dream?"

Daz said, "Before I tell you about it, I need to ask you a question. Do you believe Jesus died for your sins?" Jeff took a puff on his cigarette and said, "No," with the same expression on his face that Daz had seen in his dream. The other friend agreed. Nope. Daz said, "Well, either I'm crazy or Jesus is Lord of the universe." The friend thought about it for a minute and said, "I don't think you're crazy."

Daz describes this as his first encounter. He says that several months later a verse from the book of Romans began to come to him, a verse he remembered from his childhood: "With your heart you believe and are justified, and with your mouth you confess and are saved."[4] Daz had been, in his words, "inoculated" by his religion growing up, but he had had no idea, really, who Jesus was. Now he was at the point where he could say, "Jesus is the cosmic king, the Lord of the universe. He is my Lord."

It had been a long brokenness. Daz had been broken as a teenager in Sydney. But in Aswan, Egypt, of all places, he was broke. The two experiences were not disconnected. One led to the other. Daz still had a long way to go, years of study and prayer and relationships and discipleship. Daz is now a deeply committed church leader and follower of Jesus. And a dear friend to Lesa and me. We are awed by his faith and learn something from him every time we're with him.

I don't know what to do with Daz's story of God's intervention in his life in Aswan other than to receive it at face value. God does whatever God chooses to do. I'm grateful. I am struck by the fact that the images and Scriptures in his dream, and in the following months, were images and Scriptures of his childhood religion, of home and church and school, which had not meant much to him at the time. But somehow, they had threaded through his life, through his adolescent traumas, through the years of darkness. And then the images and Scriptures reappeared in the moment when he was, in God's good timing, receptive to God's intervention. "God puts his word upon our hearts," the old rabbi said, "so that when our hearts break, the first thing that enters is the word of God."

"Broken" led to "broke." Being hurt, wounded, torn, and lost led to surrender. Like a horse that submits, that allows himself to be conquered, tamed, ridden. And useful. Like a stone hewn from the nearby hills, cut with a clear purpose and used for a task that would last beyond a lifetime.

A question hangs over this story. The farther we go in our conversation, the more pressing it's going to become: Where is God in all this? It's tempting to answer, well, that's obvious: God was in the dream. But that's not right. We must not confuse means with end. From the beginning of the story to its climax, from childhood to adulthood, in the long brokenness and through the moment of surrender to now, the answer is the same. Where is God? God is in Daz.

Several months ago, Daz went for a walk. He heard someone behind him shouting, "Darren! Darren!" Not many people in his life called him Darren. He spun around. It was Jeff. They had lost touch with one another. It had been years since they were last together. They spent a little time catching up. Jeff now has daughters, growing up into mature women. Lately, the girls have been asking their dad about religion. Jeff has told them, "I know a guy . . ."

~

As the old rabbi from Poland had said, "There is nothing more whole than a broken heart." I must have been awfully whole. My heart and every other part of my body felt broken. I should have been more prepared. It was the spring of 2007, and I was a mess.

My story of brokenness is mine alone. Every story of brokenness belongs to the teller, not the hearers. The hearers of such stories bear responsibility for protecting the image of God in the one who is broken, whoever they may be, whatever may have happened. I share my story without a lot of detail in order to put a canvas in front of us—not a blank canvas but a sort of painting template for your own story. Not a traceable template because your story will have its own form and palette.

My story of brokenness can't be told without reference to tears. I have always had a melancholy streak. At first, I just had to live with it, sometimes with embarrassment. Eventually, I came to embrace it. When I was a boy, tears would often stream down my cheeks when I played the piano, whatever the piece was, whether a requiem, a waltz, or Chopsticks. When my summer ministry in St. Louis came to an end, the congregation presented me with a Bible. It was a small token. Very thoughtful, very sweet, but probably not deserving of the humiliating public blubbering that ensued. I vowed to never let that happen again, a vow that was impossible to keep.

I never considered taking a date to a movie that I knew would be sad. Not after watching *Love Story* my sophomore year in college with a girl I was interested in. At the end of the movie when—spoiler alert—Jenny lay in a hospital bed asking Oliver to hold her tightly as she died, I totally lost it. I tried without success to stop my heavy, wet sobbing. My date, without a tear in her eye, looked at me in utter horror. We waited until everyone left the theater before getting up out of our seats. The relationship didn't make it. I needed to control my crying in public, but I thought she needed to at least feel a little sad at a sad movie, though I later wondered if her occasional tissue wiping during the movie might, in fact, have been due to something other than the head cold she complained about. And just for the record, I did not cry when Jenny, then Oliver, said the movie's most famous line, "Love means never having to say you're sorry." That one triggered my gag reflex.

I felt like my feelings of melancholy over the years were generally controllable. I could turn them on and turn them off. Mostly. I mean, not with piano pieces, public partings, or sad movies. Or sometimes TV commercials, comedy shows, and professional wrestling. My tears, I told people, I told myself, were good. They were part of my art—my music, my words, my creativity. I didn't want to lose them. I still don't.

But one day, I couldn't turn them off. I couldn't stop crying. Not for weeks. I functioned okay during the day and cried most of the night. I lost fifty pounds in six months. My family was supportive. Work associates were encouraging. Three professionals in particular, all dear friends, provided the critical interventions I needed—my physician, who walked me through the meds; my counselor, who helped me come to grips with the underlying causes; and my pastor, who served as my priest, speaking on God's behalf to me and speaking on my behalf to God.

I have not come close again to what I experienced in those six months. Depression is real and should be taken seriously. There are many causes and many treatments. I believe in counseling and the right medications. Too many people choose not to get help. Men, in my experience, are the worst. Many of them have a hard time admitting they have a problem such as depression, and if they ever admit it, they tend to try to handle it themselves.

After my bout with depression, a sort of sixth sense emerged in me, a new awareness, a new empathy, a kind of internal radar for folks struggling with depression. Some knew they were depressed but were hiding it or brushing it aside. Some hadn't yet figured it out. I began talking to men very candidly about my experience. I walked alongside several individuals as they sought the help they needed.

Walking with friends who were experiencing depression became an unexpected ministry. It was ad hoc, informal, and sporadic. And also unsought. I would never have sought it because I would never have chosen to go through the hell I endured to obtain the perspective or the skills I needed to do it. At the same time, I know that walking with these friends was helpful—to others but also to me. I don't mean to say I think God caused my depression. I doubt it. Then again, I'm a doubter. I simply don't know. I'm more aware than ever that a hidden God does hidden things in hidden ways. But this ministry certainly began to appear after my depression. Maybe God was sending these people to me. Maybe it was just the circumstance—people who share similar problems often hang together and learn from each other.

Or maybe, just maybe, these people, or others like them, had been in my life all along and I simply hadn't seen them. Or didn't care. Maybe my brokenness opened my eyes. Maybe it opened my heart. Maybe I was beginning to live with my antennae up. I had much to learn. I was broken. But I wasn't yet broke.

~

There was no single moment when broken became broke in my life, when belief became surrender, but one early morning at IHOP came close. I was in a new city. I had a new job in a new profession. I joined a new church, the kind of church where worshippers shout, where children dance, and where justice melds with mercy in the hearts of the people. Everything was new. My brokenness was six years distant, but inside me it was still new every morning. My depression had largely been tamed. But I hadn't been. The broken places were still raw and festering.

I sat down with my pastor one morning over pancakes. He loved pancakes, though not as much as he loved grits. He had grown up in North Carolina, where grits are considered one of the major food groups. I had not tasted grits until I was in my thirties, which was astonishing to him. He told me about a friend who wanted to try grits for the first time, but when the friend placed his order with the waitress, he asked her if he could have a grit. A grit? She looked at him incredulously. You'd like a grit? Yes, he told her. I'd like to try a grit. So, whenever my pastor and I had breakfast together, he would always ask if I wanted a grit that day. Not today. Today was pancakes.

He asked me how things were going. I told him they were okay. Well, maybe less than okay. Life was busy. I shared with him some of the stresses of work, not just the ordinary demands of a stressful job but the heartbreak of poverty that I experienced every day and the dismay I sometimes felt as I realized how many advantages I had in life. I told him that church was sometimes hard, that I didn't know where I fit yet, that I found myself standing at the back when I came in, trying to figure out who to sit by. I didn't know the people well. I didn't know how my gifts and passions could be used by this church family. I was still mostly an outsider. Sometimes, I told him, I felt really alone.

We were silent for a few minutes. He began to share some stories about the congregation, things that everyone in the church family knew, pretty much everyone except me—members who had lost jobs, women who lived with abusive husbands, families who had had children murdered, members who had spent time in prison, kids at school who came home almost every day with stories of racial prejudice or racist taunting, and literally every single member of the church family who was impacted by life-sucking, exhausting, everyday racism. He took a sip of coffee, paused a couple of beats, looked up at me, and said three life-altering words:

"You got nothin'."

Perspective can be hard to come by. You have to work for it. Sometimes you have to fight for it. And sometimes you never find it. But maybe it will come, without any warning, over breakfast at IHOP, like a grit, a single grit, welling up from the inside, making your body shake as the absurdity of it all starts to become clear, the piddly little anxieties, the feeling-sorry-for-yourself annoyances, all beginning to push up through your chest, emerging into your mouth, first as a grimace, then a groan, then erupting into a belly laugh spilling out into a room full of diners, who are drinking coffee and eating buttermilk pancakes and sausage links, beginning to stare at the booth where two men, one Black and one white, are now shrieking with laughter, tears running down their faces, reveling in the truth that was already beginning to change my heart. I got nothin'. I got nothin' to complain about. I got nothin' to feel despair or anger or resentment about. I am not a victim of anything or anyone. I am blessed. God is good. And everything, indeed, was new.

When we finally gained a measure of composure, I said to my friend, I don't fully trust my own judgment right now. I'm still upside down and need to get right side up, but I can't do it myself. I need your wisdom. I need your holiness. I need your faith. I want people to see Jesus when they see me. I'm tired of trying to manage it myself—my faith, my discipleship, my future. So, I place my life into your hands. You are God's man. You are God's priest to me. Lead me. Stop me. Push me. Compel me. Whatever you tell me to do, I will do. He did. And I did. And that became our relationship for the next four years. I had surrendered to something greater than I was, not my pastor but my God. Utterly. Finally.

In those years, those hard, good years, I began to see glimpses of God in surprising places, not merely out there but within. God began to give me contentment, patience, a quieter spirit, a joyful heart, and new life. I could tell. I could see it. I just had to be broke first.

~

There's a third way. I've known this truth for a long time. I was taught it. I studied it. I shared it with congregants and students. But that's different than actually living it. This third way is a surprising way. It doesn't make a lot of sense on the surface. But it's true. The other two ways are dead ends.

The first road is the way of signs, the way of power. We've seen how that works. If only we could show others God's great power. If only Jesus would show me a sign. Surely demonstrations of power could make a big difference in our public witness. The world would be touched. They would see, and then they would believe.

The sign-seeking folks in the church in Corinth were especially concerned that the crucifixion story would not make a good first impression on prospective converts. It just wasn't a good look, the whole Son-of-God-dying-on-a-cross thing. Besides, for Jews, the notion of being put to death for a capital offense and hung on a tree was a symbol of shame, according to the book of Deuteronomy.[5] Such a person was considered cursed. Maybe we could tell folks about the crucifixion later in the process—you know, underplay it a little, especially with our fellow Jews. It just wouldn't be a good way to get their attention, to draw them in. It would be much better to give them a sign, show them a miracle. A good healing or speaking in tongues oughta do it.

The second way is the way of knowledge. Knowledge, as we have seen, gives us significant advantages. We can research and understand and then share with others what we have learned. In a city filled with wise teachers, as Corinth was, knowledge would be especially useful. Gaining a great depth of knowledge or wisdom—the Greek word is *sophia*—would allow us to have a more "sophisticated" presence in the world. Knowledge would make us confident. Knowledge would make us winners. We can know, we can be assured, about our experiences with God. That's the ticket. Wisdom is the way forward.

The wisdom folks in the church in Corinth, like the signs folks, were also concerned that the crucifixion story would not be a good way to lead people to Jesus, but their reasoning was different. In the Greek world, one of the most important characteristics of a god was the god's immortality. If gods were capable of dying, they wouldn't be gods. Gods are immortal. So Jesus, the Son of God, dying? Maybe we could tell the crucifixion story later, especially to fellow Greeks. Let's not lead with it. Better to show them how logical the Christian faith is, how much we know, how educated and wise we are. It would frankly be better if our founder, Paul, were a better speaker. Perhaps we should get some top-notch orator out front. A wise and brilliant speaker could do it.

First Corinthians was written to some messed-up Christians, but you and I aren't that different if you dig just a little beneath the surface.

We're messed up, all of us. Paul is getting at a universal human phenomenon. People are always looking for signs. Signs are about power, and power is always at play. And people are always looking to know. The drive to know more than others has always been part of the game. Knowledge, then and now, tends to puff people up. Both ways, when they are the primary impulse, are unhelpful, self-defeating.

But there's a third way, a way that cuts against both the impulse to power and the drive to knowledge. It may seem foolish to folks out there, Paul says, but while some of you were playing the power game and others of you were playing the wisdom game, I was telling the story about a crucified Christ. It's a scandalous story, a story of apparent weakness and acquiescence, a story of humility rather than domination, a stumbling block to the signs people and utter foolishness to the knowledge people. But the bloody, shameful death of the Son of God reveals, surprisingly, God's power and God's wisdom.[6]

God's way of doing power and wisdom seems upside down to the world. It appears foolish, harebrained, wacky, insane. God saved the world by giving up his Son? How does that make sense? But God's story is that Jesus was God and then gave up his divine prerogative. Christ surrendered his immortality in order to obtain immortality for everyone else. The one who is great is the least. The one who is first is last. To be great, you have to be a servant. Power is made perfect in weakness. When you are weak, you are strong.

It seems like crazy stuff, Paul tells them, but it's the only way it will work. Using power to get your way destroys the very thing you want, and knowledge places all the attention on you. But love, Paul says, love builds up. No matter how accomplished you are, no matter how rich you are, how educated you are, how powerful you are, if you don't love other people, you got nothin'. If you're impatient with them, if you're unkind or jealous, if you brag all the time about who you are and what you have, you got nothin'. If your knowledge or your success makes you arrogant, if you are constantly irritated, if you're always keeping score, always looking for ways to get back at the people who hurt you, then you got nothin'.

Don't lead with all the things that bring attention to yourself, to power or knowledge, prestige or success, accolades or accomplishments. Lead with brokenness—Christ's and your own. Don't focus so much of your attention on yourself but serve other people. Love others before anything else. And don't miss the point. The heart of the story is not merely that Christ was broken but that he was also broke. "Not my will," he prayed, "but yours be done." He chose surrender rather than control, service rather than applause. You can choose any number of ways forward in your life, but this is the only way that leads home.

When I was a young preacher, I was invited to speak at a conference in Indianapolis. It was good being back in the Midwest. As you know, they make great pierogies up there. The presentation went well, I thought. The crowd was responsive. They seemed engaged. Enthusiastic, even. When I finished, I felt as good about the presentation as any I had ever given. A crowd of well-wishers gathered around me afterward. Wow. I must have been especially good. Folks introduced themselves, wanted me to meet their families, thanked me for this comment or that insight. I might have been mistaken, but I thought I could detect the smell of incense in the room, the aroma of sweet self-satisfaction rising above me toward the heavens, pleasing, I felt certain, to God's nostrils.

I saw a man hanging back a little, waiting for the crowds to thin. I continued to visit with folks, and he stayed on the periphery. Finally, when most everyone was gone, I gestured for him to come talk to me. Interesting man. He introduced himself and gave me his card. He said he was part of a support group he wanted to tell me about. No, no, no, I thought. He's trying to sell me something. He's making a pitch. I don't need this now. My barriers went up. I began to look for an escape route. "I see," I responded. "What sort of group?" My eyes were scanning the room. Somebody, help me.

"It's a one-step group," he told me. That was not what I expected. I had heard of twelve-step groups, but this was new. He had set the bait and I bit. "I haven't heard of a group like that," I said, a little bemused. "One step, you say? What's the step?"

He looked straight into my eyes: "Step down."

The comment was sobering. He nailed me. There was nothing, really, that I could say. It may be as good a parallel as any to the contrast between broken and broke. There's a difference between stepping down and being pushed down. Or even slipping and falling. We're going to find ourselves on the ground no matter what—whether by sheer clumsiness, someone else's malevolence, or some life circumstance over which we have no control. But stepping down willingly—as an act of selflessness, humility, and trust—is a different matter altogether.

We have traveled down a couple of roads that lead to a dead end—one is about signs, the other about knowledge. Both ways have some things to commend them. They're not evil, but they can lead us off course. They offer the illusion that we're in control. They end up blocking us from the destination we seek.

There's a third way. Admitting your brokenness gets you on the road. Being broken makes you humble. It helps you choose not to judge others. It keeps you from thinking you know more than you do. But it's not enough, not if broken is to become broke. Something is still missing. Something our faith in a crucified Christ has been leading us to. It's not complicated. It just takes one step.

for

At some point, we have to ask ourselves what our faith is ***for****. Faith doesn't offer us a blanket to hide under, to protect ourselves. It doesn't insulate us from the eyes of our neighbors. We are God's gifts, God's signposts for others. We are the only face of God that many will ever see.*

09

THE GOD OF THE PERIPHERY

"Aren't you going to go out and support him? He's a 'Christ-er' like you."

I had never heard that epithet before. "Christ-er." I was taken aback. I was a grad student at a state university, working hard to do well in my courses. I was also a TA, a teaching assistant. And I was a part-time youth pastor, so my weekends were often filled with church stuff.

I had probably allowed my busyness to keep me from engaging in the life of the graduate community as I should have. On most Monday nights, after my evening class was over, several of the students and a couple of the faculty would go to a nearby pub for chicken wings. I never went. I didn't know the others very well. And I had classes the next day that I needed to be ready for.

One morning, as I rode my bike to my departmental building, I saw several folks gathered around a guy speaking loudly on top of a little wooden box. The crowd wasn't particularly big, but the guy was preaching hard at them. Loud voice. Big gestures. I felt embarrassed. I could see the impact of his behavior on the students walking by. They were headed to their classes with heads down, eyes averted. I made a wide berth around him, headed into my building, and walked up the stairs to my TA office.

My officemate had already arrived. He was an older graduate student. A little gruff around the edges, but he was all right. I didn't see him much or know him well. He was standing at his desk, looking out the window at the commons area where our would-be evangelist was really going at it, while the little crowd of spectators had dwindled to a handful. I set my backpack on my desk and sat down. I had a class to prepare for.

"Aren't you going to go out and support him?" he asked me. "He's a 'Christ-er' like you."

I could feel the blood rush to my face. "I'm not like that," I told him, sounding more defensive than I intended.

"Aren't you a Christ-er?" he asked again.

I felt paralyzed. I didn't want to be associated with the guy out on the lawn. At the same time, I didn't want to deny my faith. Visions of the apostle Peter briefly flitted into my brain—out in the high priest's courtyard after Jesus's arrest when a servant girl asked him, "You aren't one of this man's disciples too, are you?"[1] I pushed the thought away and muttered, "I'm just not like that," and I buried my head in a book.

I thought of that encounter for days. The audacity of the street preacher. What a terrible witness. Boy, had he missed the point. He was making life difficult for the rest of us believers. We were the ones having to bear the consequences of such a boneheaded display of faux discipleship. He should have been more prudent, more tactful, more strategic. Like me.

Later that week, one of my professors asked if I would step into his office. I liked this professor, though I didn't know him well. We chatted a bit, then he spoke very directly: "I'm a Christian." He wasn't asking me a question. I nodded. He was a kind man but had never talked about his faith to me before. That's not unusual. He was a professor at a state university. Separation of church and state and all that. "And I assume you're a Christian," he said, "because you have a job at a church." I swallowed. He oversaw all the teaching assistants. He had access to our files. "Yes sir," I said.

"This is a hard place to be a Christian," he told me. "I'm hoping you'll step up. You rarely hang out with the others. Your officemate tells me he never sees you. You're in your classes, then you leave. I get it. But we need to see you. The department needs to see you. Don't be embarrassed to be a Christian. I'm here for you. You can come by anytime."

My professor had gently and firmly turned my storyline on its head. I had been the smug one, the unaware one, the one who would never embarrass Jesus or myself. Especially myself. I would never be like that street preacher. I felt, and still feel, that he was sullying the name of Jesus up there on his soapbox. I just hadn't seen how I was doing something similar—not by saying too much but by being absent. By having no voice and no witness.

That's not exactly true. I was having a witness. I did have a voice. I seemed to be saying to my fellow students and faculty, "I don't see you. I don't need you. I don't care." That wasn't my intention. I just had my own life. Outside of courses and study, I was going to church and doing ministry. I was engaged in what I thought were important things. I had friends. But I wasn't looking. I didn't see. I didn't show up. I isolated myself. I missed it. He wasn't asking me to step down—that was another context and a different message—but to step up, to take responsibility. That conversation has lingered at the edge of my awareness for much of my life. What am I to do with it?

~

We began our journey here with the IF of our faith, the doubts, the hard questions that can both make faith difficult and propel faith forward. Then we lived in the WHILE, in the off-centered space between the now and the not yet. But don't get lost in some arbitrary notion of sequence. It's not like IF, WHILE, and FOR are a series of steps or stages. As if coming to grips with the doubt in the IF allows you to grow spiritually in the WHILE, and then, perhaps in the latter years of your life, you can focus on what your faith is FOR. That's like saying, "That was a hard workout. Glad I won't ever have to do that again." Or, "I was surprised at my diabetes diagnosis. Thank God for that shot of insulin." Some things are ongoing. Some things we deal with all our lives.

Beginning in 2020, a new set of health conditions, part of our post-pandemic world, was coined: "long COVID." What we're talking about here is "long faith." In all honesty, there is no other kind. Faith is protracted, stretched, complex, tangled, and thick. Faith has to juggle the IF, the WHILE, the FOR, and every other metaphor one might employ, all the time and all at once.

Sometimes faith can feel easy. Praying comes without prompting. Trusting God feels as easy as rolling down a slick hill. God seems close, accessible. At other times faith is grueling, agonizing, confusing. You feel like giving up. Trusting can be tiresome and sometimes exasperating. Even late in life, perhaps especially late in life, we recognize that the problems our faith has presented us haven't all been resolved. The questions haven't all been answered. And so, long faith is relentless. It has to be. Long faith is enduring and stressful and wonderfully fulfilling. Long faith is complicated and exhilarating. Recognizing the FOR of our faith means knowing faith's purpose and meaning, discerning what's important, and choosing to serve a cause larger than we are.

We can't push the FOR back till later when we're better prepared. I wish we could. It seems like it would be easier that way. But waiting until we think we're ready stifles or suffocates our faith. We can't afford to wait until our faith is sufficiently mature before we discover that, one way or another, what we believe and how we live have an impact on others. We don't have that luxury. We don't live in isolation. Our faith isn't shielded from the eyes and experiences of our neighbors, coworkers, friends, adversaries, and children.

A lot of Christians talk about faith as if faith is primarily about ourselves, about seeing the working of God within each of us or at least in relation to the people we care about. When we talk about knowing God or seeing God, we usually describe it in the first person. Our glimpses of God often look something like: Our worship was great this morning; I really felt God's presence in my heart. Or, I had to choose between this job or that; God prompted me to choose this one, and boy, has God blessed me. Or, my aunt Lula was sick; it looked grim; I prayed, and she got better. Or, I love seeing waterfalls and forests, the beauty of nature. I feel closer to God out there.

Great. Fine. That's part of it. But if such expressions of faith are all we have, they feel awfully self-regarding, as if God's role is mostly to make sure I'm okay. God cares how we're doing, of course, but don't miss the point. My faith isn't mine. It doesn't belong to me. Faith has an outward-oriented face, connecting us to two groups. Faith is given to faith communities, not isolated individuals. We are, or should be, accountable to a people. But there's another piece. My faith inhabits the world I live in. It impacts the people I interact with and a lot of people I don't. Others will see God by observing how we live, what we say, how we carry ourselves, and whether we show up. We are the only face of God that many will ever see.

Whether our faith is seen by others is not a choice we can make. We can't toggle the "faith" key on our keyboards from "private" to "public." We can't carry an "Off Duty" sign around our necks. Faith is always public. We can talk all we want about seeking God, listening to God, longing for God, or aching for God. We can embrace a still-enchanted universe where God is here with us, where there are thin places and thin moments between the divine and the human, where God is still at work, where God's presence is still visible. That sort of faith is not wrong or meaningless. It's good and right. Coming upon signposts from time to time is no small thing. They remind us of the journey we're on and of the destination we seek.

But we must not miss the larger point. While faith includes living with our antennae up, always prepared to see signposts of God whenever we run across them, it is much more. We don't just come across signposts from time to time so that our own walk of faith can be strengthened. We are signposts of God for others. We are a means, sometimes the only means, by which others are able to see God. The question is, what kind of God do they see when they see us? If other people are going to encounter the glory of God through us, we better ask some questions about the kind of God we think we serve, the kind of God that our worship, our conversations, our beliefs, and our behaviors exhibit to the world.

~

The glory of God is a funny thing. It doesn't show up on demand. Rarely when we want it. Sometimes not at all. If God's glory does show up, it doesn't typically come with a marching band or a drone light show. Rather, the glory of God tends to be seen in unexpected places. Like a piddly little province in a troublesome corner of the Roman Empire. Or in an animal trough amid the smell of hay, sweat, and dung. Or at a baptism in a murky Jordan River. Or as a carpenter-turned-rabbi is chased out of a synagogue for being too inclusive, telling the home crowd that God loves gentiles too. Or as nails are pounded into his wrists and feet during a scandalous execution. Odd displays of the glory of God.

God's glory apparently needs a marketing agent. At the very least, it deserves a new mission statement. And probably some updated strategies and a plan for executing and tracking the whole process. One would think God would know how to get the word out better. It's like the two friends walking back to their little village. They encountered a stranger. It was the Son of God. He was right there, walking with them. But they didn't even recognize him. That's just poor advance planning. Only when the Son of God broke bread did they identify him, and then he tucked his glory into his back pocket and was gone.

That's not the sort of glory many of us are looking for. The hidden kind. The sporadic kind. The painful kind. We'd prefer a more glorious glory, thank you. A big glory. An unending glory. Or at least something more predictable. And definitely more pleasant. We like our glories to be grand. And conspicuous. And about us. But a primary focus on ourselves and people like us—the ways I see God, the ways God helps me and my friends and my family—ends up making God small. It warps our understanding of what God is like. Our views of God are typically filtered through what we need, what we like, where we want to go, what we want to do, which are the things we most often pray about. But God uses a different set of filters.

The prophets of Israel give us a pretty good idea about what God cares about. Israel's worship was a window into the hearts of the people, and God seemed not to be happy with their worship. On one occasion, God sat through a worship service and then headed to the senior pastor after the last amen and said, "I hate, I despise your festivals, and I take no delight in your solemn assemblies."[2] Wow. Harsh words. What went wrong? Were the song choices that bad? Did the preacher screw up the exegesis? They needed to be happier, perhaps?

At another service, God stuffed a note afterward in the complaint box: "Bringing offerings is futile; incense is an abomination to me . . . even though you make many prayers, I will not listen."[3] What could have gotten God so upset? Why wouldn't God accept their praise and sacrifices? Were they offering lambs when they should have been sacrificing doves? Incense, maybe, had a pungent smell? Prayers getting off topic perhaps? No, the priests seemed to handle all that okay.

So why did God reject their worship? Not because they were doing things wrong. In fact, they seemed to be doing everything right. The problem wasn't their liturgy. It was their lives. It was their sight. Or rather, their lack of it. They didn't see the people God saw and didn't love the people God loved.

"Seek justice," Isaiah told them; "rescue the oppressed; defend the orphan; plead for the widow."[4] Micah urged them to "do justice and to love kindness and to walk humbly with your God."[5] The problem was that Israel's worshippers were focused on themselves, on their own advantages and opportunities. The people at the center of things were getting wealthy, but God's heart wasn't homed in on the wealthy, the people in power. It was with the people at the periphery of society—the outsiders, the wounded, the sufferers. When Israel overlooked them, they overlooked God's heart. Israel's worshippers weren't pursuing justice at the margins, for the ones being treated unjustly, and that was unacceptable. They were not being agents of God's grace.

At the very end of the book of 1 Peter, there is a remarkable affirmation and challenge: "I have written this short letter to encourage you and to testify that this is the true grace of God."[6] It's not terribly surprising that this letter, or any New Testament letter, ends with a line about grace. Grace is good. Grace is always welcome. But in this context, God's grace doesn't just point to all the good things God has done but to all the suffering they're going through. What an odd move.

Suffering is mentioned in almost every paragraph of the letter. The letter opens with a word about God's power, which was protecting the church through their faith. But then this surprising turn: so "you rejoice, even if now for a little while you have had to suffer various trials."[7] What kind of trials? At the very least, these Christians were being maligned, beaten, abused, and harmed.[8] But that shouldn't be shocking. Christ suffered, so you shouldn't be surprised if you suffer too.[9] So, rejoice. The letter mentions suffering every few sentences all the way to the final exhortation: Be "steadfast in your faith, for you know that your brothers and sisters in all the world are undergoing the same kinds of suffering. And after you have suffered for a little while, the God of all grace . . . will . . . restore, support, strengthen, and establish you."[10]

This, then, is the true grace of God. Suffering. But not just suffering in general. Grace is not about living a wretched life of anguish and affliction, but suffering for God's sake, like Christ did. Suffering with Christ is God's generous gift to us: You are a follower of Jesus, so congratulations! You get to suffer. Talk about grace coming at you sideways.

But it's more. To miss this is to miss the gospel. God's true grace doesn't just come at you sideways—at unexpected times, in unexpected ways, from unexpected directions. Rather, sideways is also the direction grace flows. To live in God's grace is to share with Christ in the suffering of others. Grace flows away from centers of power, toward the margins, out at the edge where God dwells.

~

In every culture, every nation, every epoch of history, there are some who have "power-up" roles and some who are "power down." The power-up people tend to be in charge, whether by the positions they hold or because of their personal influence and social advantages. People work for them or are drawn to them. They go to them for information or decisions or help. The power-down people have less influence. Often they have none. They don't have much of a voice, not because they're not speaking but because, no matter what they may say, others are not listening or don't care.

Power-up people in our society are generally good at controlling what's going on around them. They may not even think about it. Power just flows to them. They expect opportunities and seize them when they arise. They're used to the attention and the rewards of power. But people in power-down roles have fewer choices, fewer opportunities. The voices of the most powerless in our communities are often muffled. Or silenced altogether.

A lot of popular books and sermons about faith these days focus on all the good things our faith brings us. If you trust God, you'll get lots of blessings, powerful blessings, wonderful blessings, sometimes luxurious blessings. If you just look for the blessings, if you expect them and have faith, you could get yourself some. I hear this language all the time. As if that's the purpose of faith. As if that's the advantage of a relationship with God—getting something really good. As if God will open whatever doors are necessary to get you what you've always wanted.

We were out looking for houses, someone might say, and we just couldn't find anything we liked. But then we came across this amazing home. It was out of our price range, but it had everything we wanted. It was perfect. We offered less than they were asking, but they accepted it. God did that. God wanted us to have that home.

Well, maybe. Maybe so. Or it may be that what we got is simply what we wanted. Either way, be thankful. Everything we have belongs to God anyway. Always be thankful. But be careful about assuming that the things you want came to you because God wanted you to have them.

The language we use about faith's blessings often leans hard toward the power-up folks. Why do God's opportunities and blessings keep coming to people who already have so much wealth and so many advantages? God feels, in these stories, a little like a divine Santa. Be really good. Work hard. Dream big. And God will give you what your heart desires. But is that how it works? I mean, in God's economy is that how blessings are distributed? I struggle to see past the disproportionate benefits.

A Kenyan villager, a Christian leader in his area, was asked to join a mission team in nearby Tanzania. He believed it was a calling from God for which he was uniquely prepared. To pay for his training and move, he sold his cow, which would be valued at approximately $368 today. That's nice, you say. Less than $400, but that's nice. Let me put it differently. The villager cashed in all of his equity, selling the equivalent of a full year's salary and his primary way of earning an income, sacrificing everything—not just his livelihood but sources of milk, status, dowry, and security, far more valuable than a full year's income—all for the mission God had given him. But hey, at least I got the big house I wanted, the one on the cul-de-sac with the swimming pool, and for such a great price. God is good!

Enjoy the home. Truly. I say that without cynicism. Enjoy it. Use the pool with gratitude and thanksgiving. Give the house and everything in it for the use of God's kingdom and for the sake of God's glory, and do so without guilt. Just don't overlook the larger picture. Open your eyes and see people who are not like you, the ones who don't have your advantages, the power-down people whom God sees and loves.

I know the Kenyan villager. His name is David. He would not likely be able to buy lounge furniture for the swimming pool at the new home on the cul-de-sac, but he's willing to give the full measure of his financial worth so that he can be faithful to God's calling on his life, so that he can bless his family and his village and the kingdom. David doesn't see himself as living at the edge. That's culture's perspective. David is smack dab in the heart of God's kingdom. His life overflows with God's blessings. He's saturated with grace. Thriving. Joyful. My faith pales in comparison.

God's glory shows up in unexpected ways. I want to always be open to it. But the reason God may not be as visible to me as I wish is that I keep assuming that the blessings flow upriver where the powerful people live. Every now and then, God gets my attention.

~

Several years ago, I stopped at a yield sign at a busy intersection, waiting for a break in the traffic. The car behind me didn't stop in time and bumped me. I walked back to check things out. There was some damage. Not a lot, but a little. I talked to the driver. Her car was old and pretty beat up. I told her that since she had hit me from behind, she would likely get a ticket. Why don't we just put our insurance companies in contact with each other to take care of things that way? She said no, she'd rather a police officer come.

As we sat in our vehicles waiting, car after car slowed down as the drivers shouted to me, only to me, "You okay?" Some were people I knew. Some were not. No one asked about the darker-skinned woman in the old car who had run into me or called out to see if she was all right. A car pulled over, and the former mayor of our city leaned out the window. I knew him as an administrator at my university. "Are you okay?" he asked. "Anything I can do for you?" No, everything will be fine. As he drove away, another car pulled to the side of the road. The current mayor of the city stepped out. It must have been Mayors' Day. "Are you all right?" he asked. "You're not hurt?" No, thank you though.

A motorcycle officer finally arrived. He came to my car first and asked what happened. I told him the story and asked him to please be easy with the other driver, that the damage was no big deal. The officer was with her for a little while and came back to my car. "She doesn't have insurance," he told me. "I gave her a citation for the accident and another one for not having proper insurance." My heart sank. Then he said, "By the way, I was in a Bible class you taught several years ago. You wouldn't remember me. I still think about the things you taught. I just wanted to thank you." Talk about advantages.

I was just a driver in a small accident on a normal working day, but all the concern and all the love and all the power flowed away from the woman. All of it came to me.

In the days that followed, several people asked about me. Hearing that I was not hurt, they said things like, "Thank God" or "What a blessing" or "God was with you; that could have been worse." Is that what a blessing is? Not a single person asked about the woman. She received two traffic citations, which she possibly didn't have the money to cover, and had to watch as cars stopped, as people made sure the white guy with all the advantages was okay. Had God blessed me? I don't know. I wonder how God saw it.

~

Scripture is not silent about power up and power down. One of the pillars of good biblical interpretation is to read Scripture "from the bottom up," that is, through the eyes of the original readers, not our own. In the New Testament, those are people at the lower end of Roman and Greek societies. They were in the power-down positions.

A few first-century Christians had positions with some status, but most did not. Christians were often looked at warily, skeptically, distrustfully. In most places, they were at the bottom of the social order and were often considered offensive, even repulsive. No wonder these followers of Jesus sometimes referred to themselves as aliens, strangers, or exiles,[11] terms of derision that they wore as a badge of their faith.

Most of us, very likely all of us, have moved into a social status that the earliest Christians couldn't have imagined. In comparison to those days—and perhaps even in comparison to a few years ago—we've moved up. We've propertied up, statused up, powered up, and wealthed up. When we read biblical texts, we tend to do so from the perspective of people in charge, people with standing, people in nice neighborhoods, people with connections.

In our positions of relative power, wealth, and comfort, we often miss the injustices taking place in our own communities. Power-up people often have a hard time even seeing power-down communities, and so we miss the gospel at our doorsteps. People tend to form their view of God based on the behaviors of the people who claim to be God's children. If others see a God who blesses only the privileged, then who's responsible for painting such a distorted picture of God's nature?

I've described my work with a nonprofit organization addressing economic injustices in one of the lowest-income zip codes in my state. Early in that work, I went to a meeting in the neighborhood. A couple of the residents asked me how long I was going to be there. I looked at my watch, calculating when I was due to return home. "No, no," they said. "How long are you going to be here? Most white folks come here for a few days. Or weeks at the most. It's too hard for people like you. How long are you going to be here?" I couldn't bear to be seen that way. Or to let them down. I was committed to the long term.

I served in neighborhoods where many key decision-makers in the city truly did not see the residents. Literally did not see them. Here's one example among more than I can count. Beginning in the 1950s, interstate highways and other expressways were being built all over the United States. In city after city, the planners took care not to split neighborhoods, to make sure that residents could easily navigate into and out of their communities while still allowing the flow of traffic on the new highways. At least for some neighborhoods.

In my city, like most other American cities, roads were built in a way that respected the established neighborhoods. Residents had access to their grocery stores, service stations, and churches. Expressways had exits at every major intersection so folks could easily get around. In many places, the expressways were buried below the sightline, with neighborhood streets crossing over the highway every block or so. But not in every neighborhood.

In other, less affluent, less white parts of town, the highways were built as if they were laid on barren countryside—miles and miles of concrete throughways on top of city land as if no one lived there, as if no homes or stores or churches or humans were there, as if there were no neighborhoods, no one that mattered. Exits were placed miles apart because travelers, you understand, weren't expected to get off the highways in these parts of town. Nothing important there. Nothing to see. No reason to buy anything, not in these neighborhoods. These long stretches in the city were just for passing through.

Communities full of people with black and brown faces were not visible to the planners, and so these neighborhoods and neighbors were divided by the newly built highways, which often cut close-knit communities in two. And with crossovers miles apart, they couldn't get to the other side of their old neighborhood. People were cut off from stores, family members, work, and churches. In some cases, grocery stores were mere yards away, but a highway had been built in between. Years later, people without cars, which is a large portion of the neighborhoods, still have to take buses to get their groceries, often taking more than an hour to get to the store and the same for the return. Without a car, how many sacks of groceries do you think they can carry with them, climbing onto a bus, fishing coins or tokens or cards from their pockets for the ride, and then finding a place to sit? Let's assume they can carry enough bags onto the bus to have groceries for two or three days. Then they have to go back and do it again and again, while people in the power-up neighborhoods shake their heads, thinking those people sure ought to eat better.

After the highways were completed, many grocery stores had to shut down, turning their communities into food deserts. But why would city officials need to worry about that? Their own neighborhoods were getting along fine. And the big donors never complained, as long as their housekeepers and yardmen could continue taking buses to tend to their well-kept homes, gardens, and pools. In the meantime, many of us drive over miles of urban highway with little awareness of the poverty and hunger and anger and hopelessness dwelling a few yards, well, below us.

I went to community meetings in low-income areas where neighbors asked city officials why it wasn't possible for their trash to be picked up every week. These neighbors rolled their trash cans out to the curb on trash days, like in every other part of the city, like Lesa and I do every Tuesday. But far too often, no trash truck came. The officials provided various explanations—bad weather, road conditions, scheduling mix-ups. The residents were always respectful. But these good citizens knew that the residents in more upscale neighborhoods had their trash picked up regardless of the conditions. Just asking, how often does your trash truck fail to come?

Over the years that I lived in that city, I heard more than a few white Christians talk contemptuously about those neighborhoods: What's the matter with these folks? Why do they live like that? They just want handouts. Giving them help just makes them lazy. Why don't they take care of themselves? These criticisms simply didn't match my experiences on the ground. The comments came from individuals who had never met even one of the neighbors but who knew for sure that their opinions about them were correct because that's what they were reading and hearing in the social-media-soaked world in which they lived.

Occasionally, some good-hearted white folks would join a ministry at their church handing out sandwiches and socks. It's not that the neighbors didn't appreciate the help. It's just that this is not the sort of support most of them needed. The helpers could hand out some food and then scurry out of the community, feeling a little better about themselves. But the causes of the residents' impoverishment, like the residents themselves, remained unseen and unknown. Not every ministry to the homeless has these consequences. Some who serve these communities see the larger story. But churches and nonprofits have got to have their eyes open.

I'm aware I have waded into a sensitive if not perilous topic area. These are fraught times. During the years I partnered with the neighbors to address the systemic causes of poverty and racism, the issues at a local level were not considered political, or at least they weren't aligned with political parties or interests. Not everyone agreed on the solutions or even the problems, and the discussions could get heated at times, but the arguments were not waged along partisan lines. By current standards, those days seem quaint. We have some hard things to consider here. Christians, of all people, should be able to talk about difficult matters through the lens of the gospel and do so without saying or doing hurtful things. In general, we're not doing so well.

In late 2024, David French, a *New York Times* opinion writer and a very public, committed Christian, wrote an article entitled "Why Are So Many Christians So Cruel?"[12] It's a question worth asking. We Christians don't see ourselves as cruel, but it's how we often act. It's what we reveal to others. French writes, "We persuade ourselves that we're not just right but that we're so clearly right that opposition has to be rooted in arrogance and evil. We lash out. We seek to silence and destroy our enemies."

A growing trend among American evangelicals is an overt opposition to the whole notion of empathy, or what some are calling "toxic empathy,"[13] which they believe is a way that political liberals are manipulating Christians to support left-wing causes: Too many Christians are just too kind; we've gotta learn to harden our hearts a little so that things can be done more efficiently. But kindness and care for others aren't partisan issues. They're central to God's heart. How could you understand the gospel apart from an overwhelming sense of generosity and concern for others? When Christians, for political advantage, lose the capacity to feel others' pain, not only is the gospel lost, but we distort the image of God to the people who see us.

Several years ago, a member of a nearby congregation asked if their church might put a little piece in the Sunday bulletin. Our city was housing several dozen young boys and girls, part of the community of refugees that had recently crossed the southern US border. The shelter was asking for help with clothes, food, and other essentials. Churches across the city put the word out. A number of the church members contributed. Several went to the shelter to help. One member, however, was outraged. He put a note in the contribution basket saying, "Do NOT give any of my money to these illegal aliens." He was so upset that a few days later he left the congregation.

These were children. They were scared. They were hungry. They were not in that city illegally. But even if they had been, it misses the point. They were children who were scared and hungry. They were humans, made in the image of God. A couple of years ago, I went with a group of ministers to visit a refugee shelter in far West Texas. It was sobering. Some of these families had escaped torture in their Central American countries. Some of them had been targeted because they were opposed to communism. Some of the boys had been recruited into gangs or threatened with their lives if they didn't join. Some had been kidnapped. Some of their friends had been killed. Some of the girls at the shelter had been raped. These refugees were receiving medical care, counseling, food, and clothing as they prepared for their hearings. We listened to their classes. We talked with their counselors. It was heartbreaking. And inspiring. Being with them, sharing a tiny bit of their suffering and their hope, was a gift of God's grace to us.

Two thoughts kept going through my head. The first was that these refugees more closely resembled the earliest Christians than I did. They were outcast and oppressed. They had suffered mightily. They had left their country mostly out of fear. Going back was not an option. That would mean reexperiencing things too horrible to imagine. But they also knew many Americans did not want them, that many Christians did not want them. They had no home, they had no country, a lot like the early Christians who also saw themselves as aliens, strangers, and exiles. I had experienced nothing in my life that corresponded to such suffering and such courage.

My second thought was, why are so many Christians so angry at them? I am not offering a partisan political argument. I understand every country needs to have border policies and enforcement. I know that some who cross the border have nefarious motives. But I'm talking about something else—our behavior, not theirs. I simply cannot grasp the harsh rhetoric coming from some Christians these days. What Christians say and how we say it has an impact. The language and attitudes of Christians say something about what we care about and believe in. Our rhetoric paints a picture of the God we serve. The view our neighbors have of God is being shaped by the way we talk and live.

If there's anything we know about God from Scripture, it's that God stands with those who suffer. God sees them and loves them. When people are abused or oppressed or ridiculed or hurt, God's heart breaks. But the image many are seeing, through the language and behavior of some Christians, is of a God who is heartless and cruel, a God who cares first about people in power, people with property, people with wealth. This too is a glimpse of God, though one that is neither accurate nor helpful.

Lesa and I have discovered a new family member, an unexpected genetic relative who has become a significant part of our lives in the last few years. When she first discovered we were Christians, she was appalled. How can you be a Christian, she asked us. Christians are so hateful. Christians are so judgmental. Christians believe that God loves America more than other nations and that God loves white people more than other races. Christians say they're about love, but I don't see much of their love.

We've tried to respond to her with a different vision of the Christian calling, an alternative picture of the God we serve, one that better reflects the witness of Scripture, one that looks like good news. But we've also had to agree with her about the Christians she has seen.

She has hung with us. She's made it clear that she isn't interested in becoming a Christian. She just wants to be with and enjoy her newfound family. We love her dearly. She loves us. Because she loves us, she asks us, in one form or another, why Christians are so cruel. The question we are asking ourselves is, What kind of God do we want her to see?

I have found myself thinking a lot about the professor who called me into his office years ago. "This is a hard place to be a Christian," he told me. It is. Life is. More than I could understand as a young man. "I'm hoping you'll step up," he said. He gave me a kick in the pants that I needed. The task before me was not to step up to more power.

God's kingdom is about relinquishing power, not seizing it. He was asking that I step up in my responsibilities. I got all that, at least at a basic level.

But the line that caught me by surprise was, "We need to see you." Why did the faculty, staff, and my fellow students need to see me? Why did anyone need to see me? I was nobody in the department. I had nothing they didn't already have. Talk about power down. I was a new student and in way over my head. This gentle, thoughtful, bold, humble professor was asking me not for hard work or well-written papers or good grades. He was asking for my presence as a Christian. Whether I chose it or not, my witness was noticeable. He was asking me to live as a follower of Jesus consciously, visibly. Not on a soapbox, not with a bullhorn, but in quiet conversations and wordless compassion with my students, my officemate, and with the community. I didn't fully understand what he was telling me at the time. It came at me sideways. I missed its importance.

I also missed how my professor was living. I didn't know until years later. He was serving people out in the community—quietly, without fanfare, at the periphery of society, which is the very heart of God's kingdom. I'm only now beginning to grasp what he was telling me. He was saying something, I think, about the true grace of God.

10

TO BRING FAMILIES TOGETHER

Her name was Mattie. I wish I had met her before she passed. She must have been something.

Her story, at least the little part I know, begins with two brothers and two plantations about two centuries before Mattie died. Samuel and Alexander Turrentine were part of a wave of Irish immigrants, around 200,000 or so, who came to the New World in the middle decades of the eighteenth century. The brothers arrived at the Port of Philadelphia in November 1745.[1]

They had financed their journey by selling the labor of their hands for a period of two years. In other words, they were, like many other Irish immigrants in the day, indentured servants. Two Pennsylvania landowners met them at the harbor, paid for the passage, and put them to work on their farms. When the terms of their indentureships were completed, the brothers each found work nearby and made a decent living until the skirmishes between the French and British caused them to join a great Irish migration south, down the Shenandoah Valley, away from the conflicts. They settled in North Carolina. There, in 1761, Samuel and Alexander were each granted acreage, a little more than a thousand acres between them, in the Little River area of Orange County, just north of what is now Durham.

Barely fifteen years after arriving in Philadelphia as indentured servants, the two Irishmen had become substantial landowners. Over the decades, the two Turrentine plantations became quite profitable. The family name was passed down from generation to generation.

There is nothing particularly unusual about the Turrentine story, unless it's how the two brothers pronounced their names. Alexander pronounced the last syllable of his last name with a long "i," as in "Valentine." Samuel pronounced the last syllable of his name like "teen." The descendants of the two Turrentine lines are phonologically split, each side preserving the pronunciation of their original American ancestor.

The far more common part of the story is that the Turrentines, like most plantation owners in the Old South, had children through their Black slaves. Though it was commonplace, the traumas it produced should not be whitewashed. In fact, the sheer everydayness of the offense only serves to amplify the horror of it. The slave women had no agency in the matter, no choice. The difference between the slaves' "power down" and the landowners' "power up" was total. The fact that it happened so often and so long ago doesn't reduce how heartbreaking it is. Many of their descendants today still bear the imprint of the original violations—on their skin, in their names, and on their hearts.

In the twentieth century, Turrentine family reunions began to sprout up from time to time. The earliest reunion that anyone knows of took place in Hillsboro, North Carolina, in 1941. It was for the white Turrentines. The second one was held in Sevier County, Arkansas, and was attended not only by white Turrentine family members from the county but also by descendants of the former Turrentine slaves of that county. So, there had been Turrentine slaves in Arkansas and elsewhere, not just at the old plantations in North Carolina. In the years afterward, the white Turrentines, who were scattered across the country, gathered every two years. The Black Turrentines, most of whom continued to live in or near Orange County, North Carolina, met together annually in a long, joy-filled time of celebration, reconnection, music, games, and remembrance, in the tradition of Black family reunions in America.

Somewhere along the way, a white member of the family, Durwood Turrentine Stokes, went to visit Mattie Clyde Turrentine at her home in Orange County. Mattie's father, Calvin, had been a slave, born in 1850. Her mother, Emmaline, was born after the Civil War. Mattie was a farmer like her ancestors. She was the unofficial and beloved matriarch of the Black Turrentines. Mattie and Durwood visited a while and shared stories of their families—of their family.

Mattie asked him if he wanted to see the headstones of the old brothers Alexander and Samuel. He did, for sure. They drove together a few miles west to an area on Hopkins Road just north of the Little River. The field was a mess, overgrown with weeds and untended to. Since the Civil War, a few Turrentine family members had been buried there—Blacks on one side, whites on the other. They walked the property for a bit, then Mattie pointed to a spot. They began pulling back the undergrowth until they uncovered the graves of the two brothers. They stood together quietly, looking at the old, simple headstones of the Irish brothers Samuel and Alexander Turrentine, their eyes filled with tears, a white man and a Black woman with different stories but common blood.

Mattie is the one who suggested that they have a family reunion of both sides of the family—not the "teens" and "tines" sides but the white side and the Black side. They did. And more than once. The family members would come together and eat, hug, play games, tell stories, and pray. These gatherings couldn't have been easy for Mattie, at least at first. Imagine having grown up a Black girl in America in the 1920s and '30s. Imagine the racist slurs she would have heard. Imagine not being able to sit down as a customer in a white-owned restaurant or shop in a white store or go to a white school or worship in a white church. Imagine the Black men she knew during the years of World War II, having to serve in separate units from whites, often cooking the food and digging the latrines for the white soldiers. Mattie would have seen and heard a lot over the years of her life.

That part of the story is hard to hear, hard to tell. By all appearances, the white Turrentines have worked hard to address their complex family story with integrity. I'm not a stranger to complex family stories. I also have ancestors who owned slaves. The thought of it remains unbearable to me. Because I know, I have responsibilities. Edward Ball, in his book *Slaves in the Family*, tells his own family story. Upon meeting Emily Frayer, a descendant of slaves owned by his ancestors and a blood relative of his, Ball asked for her forgiveness. "Yes, we forgive," she answered. "It didn't hurt me, now, but the people before me, and they all gone." Ball replied, "We're not responsible for what our ancestors did or did not do, but we're accountable for it."[2] Yes. We are accountable. I am accountable.

Mattie had not known that there were any Turrentines other than the ones in her county until her white relative knocked on her door. Now she began to seek them out. Relentlessly. For years. She didn't have to do it. She didn't have to try to push those doors open. Everyone would have understood if she just stayed out of it, living quietly on her farm. So, why did she? Why did she take the risk? She was clearly a person of faith. That had to have played a role in her commitment to the ministry of peacemaking. But it was also because they were family. Families talk. Families get together. Families love each other. This is what families do, even when it's difficult. So, she pushed against the doors, and the white Turrentines and Black Turrentines began to close the long divide between them.

In the years after Mattie and Durwood stood at the graves of their ancestors, other members of the family, upon their deaths, began to be buried in the now well-tended field, which was soon known as the Turrentine Family Cemetery. For the rest of her life, Mattie worked tirelessly to reconnect all the Turrentines that she could, both Black and white. She died in 1979 at Duke University Hospital. She was buried in the family cemetery, not far from Alexander's and Samuel's graves. Her headstone reads: Mattie Clyde Turrentine, 1910–1979, "She Who Brought Families Together."[3]

I can hardly imagine a more meaningful epitaph. Mattie's heart may have carried the imprint of the original rape that led, generations later, to her birth, but it also carried something more powerful, more compelling, more far-reaching. Mattie's heart was filled with forgiveness, with compassion, with grace, components of a salve that not only could soothe hearts like hers but could also heal the hearts of her white relatives who share her bloodline and her story.

~

With forgiveness. With grace. With her family. With.

I love prepositions. I love words, period. But my mind is constantly sorting through possible prepositions in a sentence—the right prepositions to say what I want to say. Prepositions are relationship words. They connect a noun or pronoun to another word in the sentence. As the word itself indicates, prepositions are in the "pre" position. They come before. Occasionally, you'll find a connecting word that comes after, such as "the whole night *through*" or "her claims *notwithstanding*." Those are technically postpositions rather than prepositions, but same idea. They connect.

Prepositions matter because meaning matters. Did the cat jump *in* the hat or *into* the hat? They mean different things. In the first, the action begins and ends in the hat. In the other, the jumping starts on the outside. Is Uncle Stanley *on* the ground or *in* the ground? Certainly not the same thing. Did you miss your appointment *by* accident or *on* accident? Well, one of those is correct, and the other not so much. But hey, I don't want to judge a book, you know, on its cover.

Few prepositions, though, carry as much force as the word *with*. At least in my mind. *With* is a simple word. Plain, in many ways. Common. But it can be powerful. Even life changing. I started thinking a lot about the word *with* when I was a young adolescent. (Yes, I might have been an odd child.) In elementary school, for reasons I never fully understood, I wasn't allowed to spend much time with my friends away from my own house. The less opportunity I had to be with my friends, the more important *with* became.

At church, I had to sit with my parents. I would look around and see my friends sitting together. They'd wave at me and make faces. Hard to imagine that my parents couldn't trust me. But at about age twelve, I was finally able to be with friends, to sit with them, to be in their homes, to go to the park with them, to have a measure of independence with them.

In high school, my friends and I would pile into one car or another. The legal driving age in those days was fourteen—I'm almost certain it was because of the extraordinary maturity we exhibited in those days, evidence of which I'm sure you'll discover here—and we would head to Mack's. Mack's was a drive-in hamburger joint, the kind that most towns had in the sixties. Think *Happy Days*. Kids from the two local high schools would go to Mack's every Friday and Saturday night to drive around. That's it. We drove in a circle, sometimes clockwise, sometimes counterclockwise, around one city block and then around again. Just being together. Talking. Windows down, even in the winter. Shouting at our friends. Occasionally mustering the courage to say hello to a car full of girls. The point was not to do something or accomplish something or get something. It was simply to be with each other. We were good boys. We never got in trouble. Not at Mack's, anyway. That came at a different venue about a mile away.

One day, a friend and I were headed up to the top floor of a downtown building where his dad owned an FM station. FM was brand new in those days. Hardly anyone had FM radio. The station played classical music. The three regular listeners apparently enjoyed it a lot. On our way up the elevator, someone stopped a couple of floors below the radio station and got out. As the elevator doors opened, we could see into a sizeable entrance room leading to the big, wooden front doors of a law office.

Just a glimpse of the entryway sparked our imaginations. What a great little place, we thought. We didn't want to break in. It seemed sort of like a public room. Sort of. We certainly weren't interested in going inside the law office. Besides, we knew those office doors would be locked after hours. We were focused on the entry room, which was like a little lobby with access from the elevator. What if we and some of our friends came up there some night and had a party? The more we talked, the better the idea became.

So we called a bunch of friends and arranged a little party for a Saturday night. Cokes, chips, and a portable stereo. We had planned an evening of music and merriment. About a dozen seventeen- and eighteen-year-old boys and girls learning to line dance. What could go wrong? Mostly we talked, laughed, and listened to the music—Creedence Clearwater Revival, Three Dog Night, Jimi Hendrix, Cream. We were having a blast. Good, clean fun among friends. Apparently the cops, who unexpectedly emerged from the elevator into our little party, missed the good and clean part.

We spent much of the rest of the evening with our city's finest. They asked us some very probing questions, like "What were you thinking?" Looking back, I think it was probably a good question. We got a stern lecture. They took our names and addresses. We promised to tell our parents. And we all did. We were too afraid not to. Turns out, our parents were not as amused about our little party as we were. Who could have guessed? They talked among themselves and agreed to revoke our rights to be with one another for, oh, about a decade. *With* has its ups and downs.

It came to have a whole new meaning when a fellow student died. He was loved by our high school and our city. He was an elite athlete. A quarter-miler on the track team. And he sang like an angel. He had just competed at the state track meet. Drowned in the lake next to his hotel. We were inconsolable. I was two years younger and had been on the track team at the time. I was certainly not elite, then or ever. But I had been on buses and in locker rooms with him, on the track and in the weight room. My mind could hardly grasp it. The track coach was my geometry teacher, the best math teacher I ever had. Hardly a class period passed when there were no tears.

Those are the sorts of moments when you lean on other people. It's how we were made: to grieve together, to spend time together, to ride in cars and laugh together, to listen to music and line dance together, to be accountable together, to join and learn and cherish and delight and suffer and work and share together. To bring families together, even when it's hard.

We were created to be with others, created for the sake of others. We need other people. We are better, less selfish, more aware, when we're in relationship with others and are responsible to others, especially when they are different from us. This community-nature of humans is not surprising since God, in God's essence, is a community. God's nature is revealed in the God-community—three divine persons; each fully God; each distinct; collectively, collaboratively, conjointly, existentially, and essentially one. That's the spiritual DNA that humans inherited. We, who were created by this God-community, were made with a need for others, a longing and desire for others, because community is knit into our souls.

But not simply for our own pleasure. If that were the case, just hanging out with the folks we like, or the ones who are like us, would be enough. And frankly, that's tempting. Being together and enjoying one another is good. But if the pleasure of one another's company is all we care about, it can be pretty self-centered: I'll be in your life as long as you make me happy, but if you're not fun anymore or if I don't agree with you or like how you live, then I'd rather just go my own way; I don't need people like you; you are not welcome at my table.

Our relationships with others are not about enjoyment. They're not simply about our own well-being or self-satisfaction. Relationships are designed with purpose. Christ entered our world as "Emmanuel," God *with* us, God in the flesh. But not merely to be with us. Christ came to transform us into something. In other words, God is not just with us but is WITH us FOR us. And that's what God created us to be. We are servants first. We are being molded, reshaped, day by day, into a community of care, into the suffering and renewing presence of Christ in the world.

But we're more than servants. We are windows through which others may see God. It is by our words and behaviors, by the virtues and passions God has cultivated in us, that others may glimpse God. One way or another, what we do and who we are point to God. The only question is, what kind of God? What picture of God are we portraying?

If God is largely invisible in our world, could it be, at least in part, that by the ways we speak and act, we have compounded God's hiddenness? Have Christians in our time camouflaged God, shrouded God with values we have manufactured, obscured God with ideals and behaviors that we have misconstrued as God's kingdom? Have we mistaken power for passion, judgment for courage, control for accountability, exclusion for purity, winning for righteousness? Have Christians become complicit in the dehumanization, the vengeance, and the cruelty that have become commonplace in the public life of our politics and culture? If not by our actions, then by our silence or by our tacit approval?

Christian discipleship is not an accumulation of private acts of devotion. It's about how we treat others, how we serve others, how we welcome others. So if God is community, where is the community-nature of God visible in our discipleship? How can we be the people of God's own heart if we do not see or will not love people who are not like us; people we disagree with or are estranged from; people who may anger us or repulse us; people who are frightened, desperate, in pain, not in their right minds, not making good decisions; people who are on the other team, in the other party, or who live in the other part of town? How will these people be served in the name of Jesus? How will they be transformed? How will we? How will others come to know the God who invites the people that we find difficult to a table of welcome if those same people are not welcome at our own table?

~

I was sitting about a third of the way back in the sanctuary. Actually, it was more up than back. The church was meeting in an old theater, so the rows of seats rose steeply all the way to the top. The place was crowded that Sunday morning—maybe two hundred people or so. Because it had once been a theater, recently purchased by the congregation, the acoustics were lively. The spirited greetings of the church family filled the room every week with joy and welcome, the sounds of celebration overflowing out into the nearby street. Strangers often walked into the theater-now-church to see what was going on. Some of them stayed. For years.

The church was in Nairobi, Kenya. Earlier in the week, I had been teaching at a nearby school. I was to preach at the service that morning before returning home later in the week. It's a fascinating congregation in so many ways. On any given Sunday, a number of languages were spoken among the members and visitors. While English was the common tongue, a vestige of Kenya's colonial past, many of the songs were sung in Swahili and various tribal languages. It was an honor being with them.

Shortly after the sermon, one of the ministers stood on the stage to give instructions to the worshippers. Just behind him and over to his left was a wooden table stacked with communion trays. The minister informed the congregation that several women and men would be stationed around the room, serving as prayer partners during the Lord's Supper. "We'll be singing for a while," he said. "When you're ready, come down the aisle to the stage and take a piece of the bread and drink from the cup. Consider stopping and praying with one of the brothers or sisters before returning to your seats. Take your time."

Then he turned quite serious. "Do not take communion today if there's someone in this church you are not reconciled with. Just come and stand by the table. If there's going to be reconciliation today, let it be at the table of our Lord." Then we began to sing.

It's hard to describe fully what happened next. As we sang, this family or that would get up and go to the table. Then an individual or a couple or another family. Each came to the table, gathering with other Christians, embracing, praying, taking the bread and the wine. Many would then go to one of the men or women scattered around the sanctuary and pray with them.

A family of four, sitting in the row directly in front of me, stood up and moved to the aisle—a mother, father, and teenage son and daughter. As we sang, they made their way toward the table, finding a place a little over to the side. They turned, faced the congregation, and waited.

I slid to the edge of my seat. A couple across the room stood up. Then a man in the front row, then a couple of women, now others beginning to stand, raise their hands, and pray. The whole church seemed to be holding its breath. It seemed to go on forever, but it was probably not more than a couple of minutes when a family several rows behind me stood and began making their way to the stage. They went straight to the family waiting by the table. The two men spoke for a minute or two. Then they embraced. The wives reached out and held each other, their bodies shaking, their faces wet. Then, others in the room began to join them, some running from their seats to the table to embrace the two families and pray with them. Most of the congregation was standing now. Those who were able to sing through their tears did so with greater volume and more ardent praise. The two families, arm in arm, went to the table, took the bread, and drank the wine *with* each other.

I was a limp rag. I did not know these families' stories. I did not need to. Something profound had happened. The moment was holy. God was present. I knew it. I saw it. I couldn't miss it. Afterward, I visited with the minister for a few minutes. I was fascinated by how all this was set up, by the process of it all, the prayers, the instructions, the congregation's response. I asked him, how often do you do this sort of thing?

He looked at me strangely, like, what sort of question is that, or what kind of Christian are you? He finally said, "Well, this is the Lord's Supper. We do this every week. Don't you?"

Well, yes. And no. I was part of a church family that celebrated the Lord's Supper each week. But nothing like that. I wondered what my church would be like if we did that, if we loved like that, if we knew each other like that, if we treated each other and spoke to each other and forgave each other like that. What if our table was not so much a focal point in the room upon which sat a beautifully appointed plate and chalice but more a table of reconciliation and peace? What if it were a table of welcome among a people of welcome?

~

Over time, words change because contexts and meanings change. "Welcome" is one of those words. In Old English, the word was *wilcuma*, the heart of which is the word *will*, a word we know well. To will something is to choose it, to desire or determine it. To leave a will is to determine the future of one's possessions, to name those to whom your things will belong. Willing is a matter of the mind—a choice to do or not to do, to give or not to give. But it's also a matter of the heart. *Cuma*, just like it sounds, means "to come." Come join us. Come to dinner at our house. Come into our home as our honored guest. Today, "welcome" is generally a polite response to a person's "Thank you." But at its source, welcoming is to will others or desire them to come. To welcome is to choose them, urge them, to be with you. It is to greet them as if they were family, to ask them into your home to receive your hospitality, and for you to receive theirs, not like strangers but as family.

That's why the church banner "Lost Sheep Welcome" felt so odd to me, like extending hospitality with an ulterior motive. We offer our hand of welcome to our neighbors, but it's conditional. We know the small print; they don't. We welcome them, but they will remain outsiders to us, at least until they change. Our guests will need to fix something before they can join us. Until then, they're still, really, on the outside. And if what makes them different from us cannot be changed, they simply cannot be part of us. Maybe they could be with people of their own kind but not with us. That sense of exclusiveness, of distinguishing "us" from the "other," destroys our welcome and diminishes our God. It happens far too often. Because it does, Christians cannot afford to sit back and see or say nothing.

I want to mention two examples, knowing that some may choose to see these perspectives as partisan. They are not, or at least don't have to be. But by declaring them so, detractors can have a chilling effect on even the possibility of meaningful dialogue among Christians of goodwill. And that's the point. Being with others means being able to listen and talk, even if the differences are wide and the emotions heated. In discussing these two matters, I'm asking readers to be open to two gospel behaviors: to talk with others about disputable matters peaceably and to see people who are different from you with compassion.

First, I want to acknowledge that many of the racial injuries Mattie Turrentine endured in her day—whether in words, by law, or through everyday actions—are not lived out as blatantly or publicly in our society today as they once were. But that doesn't mean they're gone. They are not. In fact, because these slights and insults are largely, though not entirely, removed from the public eye, they may be more insidious.

The church cannot afford to accept the judgment that racial and ethnic discrimination no longer exists in the United States. Or any other country. When we do, we remove the welcome from our hearts, and we distance our communities of faith from people in our cities and in our churches who are in real pain. We are saying, in essence, "It makes me uncomfortable when I'm told you are demeaned or humiliated because of your race. I'm not sure I believe it. White people are hurt too. Let's stop talking about race. I don't even see race." If only it could be true. White people in America have the prerogative of not seeing race. That's not possible for everyone.

Just in the last few weeks, I have heard multiple stories that belie the claim that racism is either nonexistent or insignificant. A Black sister told several of us that she has to be careful when she walks into a store not to be suspected or accused of shoplifting. She always keeps her hands visible. She's aware of store clerks who often follow her to make sure she doesn't steal anything. A Black city official told me that the respectful talk of his white colleagues, which is standard in public meetings, is often set aside when the officials meet in private sessions, when the camera is off, when their racist language won't be reported to their constituencies. I visited with a Mexican American friend, an American citizen, who carries multiple documents with him wherever he goes—not just his driver's license but his passport, social security card, and even utility bills—to make it less likely that the authorities will pick him up or disappear him on suspicion of his being an undocumented worker because of the color of his skin or his name. A Black friend was recently told by a clerk at the local farmer's market to go to a market on her own side of town.

In the last few years, I've heard Black children describe the racist slurs they hear on a regular basis at school. I've heard from Hispanic kids who are taunted by classmates to go back where they came from. I know African and Asian immigrants who have been told they are not wanted here. I know Black families whose homes have sold for considerably less than comparable homes owned by white families in their neighborhoods. These are not newspaper reports or stories that can be found in the dark corners of the internet. These come from people I know well. They are not uncommon.

Christians cannot, must not, turn our faces from such stories because they make us uncomfortable or because our friends might criticize us for being "political" or, God help us, "woke." We're talking about human beings, carriers of God's Spirit. Racism must not be trivialized or explained away. Christians cannot afford to play politics about racism or any other sin. No one can. If you're white, take a moment and ask your Black friends, your Hispanic friends, or other persons of color whom you know about their experiences with racism. I have little doubt about what you will hear. And if you don't know anyone well enough to ask, or aren't close enough to them that they can talk candidly to you, then perhaps the problem begins there.

We cannot be the people of welcome God calls us to be if we are not willing to hear the stories of those who are being demeaned or demoralized, or if we indicate to them that sharing their stories is political so they should stop. We cannot be the church God created us to be if we're not willing to listen to their pain, to stand with them and for them. Doing anything less is to say to the world, "Our God doesn't see, our God doesn't care," or "God sees and cares only for people like me." If that's the image of God that others have, and frankly it is for many in our society, there's no other place they could have gotten it than from the behavior of some of Christ's followers. For anyone who wonders why church attendance and belief in God are in decline, perhaps this is a good starting place.

Okay, perhaps we should pause for a second or two. Take a deep breath. Maybe get a drink of water. But we can do this. We can talk about difficult things. We have to. The church needs us to. The world needs us to. God called us to. All right, we have a second example to consider. Let's wade back in.

Brandi Carlile told a story in her memoir *Broken Horses* that ripped my heart out. In part, I felt it as deeply as I did because there was a time when it could have been a story about me. I had been a youth pastor before, like the one in Brandi's narrative. In all honesty, I wonder if I would have done or said what he did. I don't know for sure. I hope I wouldn't have. It was a long time ago for me. But mostly, I felt the searing heartbreak of watching a person damaged deeply—not just damaged but damaged in the name of Jesus.

Brandi's parents had not encouraged her to be a person of faith. Their own experiences with the church had not been great. But she had a longing, a need, an emptiness that remained unmet. She says she had been drawn for a long time to church, both as a comfort and out of fear.[4] She had gone to church camp. Her younger brother and sister had been baptized. She was a bit of a mess. She was at the edge of eighteen. It just seemed like it was time to take the same step her siblings had.

She had been in spiritual training with her youth pastor all week. He knew her. She had kept no secrets from him. On the night of her baptism, her friends and most of her family were there at the church to support her. A boy was also being baptized that night. He was thirteen. The youth pastor took both of them to a back room to get ready. Before they got in the water, he asked them, "Do you practice black magic or witchcraft?" The question took Brandi by surprise. She thought he was just making a joke to break the ice. She laughed, but the question wasn't asked in jest. She straightened up and assured him that she did not. Now she understood what was going on. She knew what the next question would be. The pastor was nervous: "Do you practice homosexuality?"

She had not kept her sexual identity from him. Everyone knew. She knew he knew. She had thought about this question many times before. She had studied the Greek words from Scripture. She had read a lot by that point. She was not uninformed. "I don't care for that word," she told him. "I'm only being who I was born to be."

The pastor told her, "I know, but I have to ask these two questions, and if you can't repent, I can't baptize you."

"What about this week?" she asked him. He had been with her all week; he had studied with her and talked with her. He knew she was gay, but he had said nothing. "I know," he said. "I'm so sorry." She ran out, and it was over.

I'm horrified by the whole story. When I heard it, I couldn't help but think about people I knew who had experienced something like it. One of my closest friends was publicly called out by his church and condemned for being gay. They did it on a Sunday morning when hundreds of out-of-town visitors were present. It was humiliating. I can't say for sure whether it was designed to be. I know ministers who have been fired because their children were gay. I know churches that have kicked kids out of their youth group, telling them not to come back to church after they revealed they were gay. I know kids who have attempted suicide after being called out by such a church. I'm aware of some suicide attempts that were successful. To say it's tragic is inadequate.

Ten years after this traumatic event in her life, Brandi made the decision, again, to be baptized. She had been reading the Bible extensively, but also modern authors like C. S. Lewis and Rachel Held Evans. She was especially moved by Brennan Manning, the author of *The Ragamuffin Gospel*, whose own life was deeply troubled—"disgraced, divorced, alcoholic," she described him. Manning wrote from his deep brokenness and touched Brandi in a way "that no pious teacher ever could have."[5] His understanding of the twenty-third psalm was particularly meaningful to her. He had written that the opening line of the psalm, the familiar but stale, "The Lord is my shepherd; I shall not want," is better translated as "I lack nothing," an insight that was transformational to her. I lack nothing. Brandi had lived a hard life, growing up in difficult circumstances and deep poverty. Now she was moving to a new understanding of God and herself. I lack nothing. Like Manning, she could finally believe in herself enough and in God enough to know that her "worthiness was irrevocable." With this new hope, she was baptized on an Easter Sunday.

But she still bore the scars of her first attempt at baptism. Even then, she says that as difficult as her first try had been on her, she wasn't mad at the youth pastor. She couldn't face him again, but she wasn't upset at him for not baptizing her. She knew she had been a mess. "I knew," she said, "that *I* wouldn't have baptized me."[6]

That's a surprising turn. I wasn't expecting that. But isn't it the point? I mean, the part about being a mess? Baptism isn't for the people who have their act together. It can't be. It better not be. Because no one has that. The whole blood of Jesus thing is for messed-up people only. The righteous need not apply.

Do you remember Jesus going to a party thrown by a tax collector? Earlier in the day, this tax collector, Levi, had been sitting in his booth ripping off his fellow citizens. Jesus apparently looked at him and thought to himself, Now that's the one I want; I'll take the tax collector, the one everybody hates. So he asked Levi to follow him. And he did. And then that night, Levi threw Jesus a big party. The place was teeming with Levi's tax collector friends and other disgraced types. A good time apparently was had by all.

Perhaps we should stop here and ask, is that any place for the Son of God to be hanging out? Is that the glimpse of God we want people to have? It's like Jesus attending a party full of petty thieves and drug addicts. Won't he hurt his reputation by hanging out with that sort? Which is pretty much what the Pharisees were saying: "Why are you eating and drinking with sinners?" But that's the point, right? "It's not the healthy people who need a physician; it's the sick," Jesus said. "I'm not here to call the righteous but sinners to repentance."[7] My question is, who are the sick people in this story? Who are the ones who need a physician? And which sinners is Jesus referring to here? Who are the ones needing to repent?

Jesus healed on the sabbath. Several times, apparently. It was against the rules, and it drove the religious leaders crazy. So he asked them, Which is lawful, "to do good or to do harm on the Sabbath, to save life or to destroy it?"[8] In other words, are our religious beliefs and practices causing death, or do they bring life? Do they lead to acts of graciousness and kindness or to condemnation and destruction? How are we known to the world around us? How do we want to be known? As the angry, finger-pointing bunch or the ones who bring families together?

I take the Bible seriously—like you, I assume. But there have always been serious differences concerning same-sex relationships among people who take the Bible seriously, not just recently but across the centuries. I know serious Christians who have serious training in theology and biblical texts who arrive at different conclusions on this issue. I can't solve it here. Ultimately, good theology will need to carry the day, and a Mattie-like heart for bringing families together, even when they're estranged. Disagreement within the Christian community is inevitable. We have to talk about things. Peaceably. And humbly. And, as Paul would remind us, not to claim we're wiser than we are.

What I'm urging here does not depend on your answer to the "is it sinful?" question. That question is not unimportant, mind you. In fact, to many individuals and families this question is crucial, decisive, even existential. And if it's important to some families, it's important to all of us. But I'm asking something different. My question is, are our gay family members and friends welcome at the table? Families are complicated. All families are. Family members don't always understand each other. Family members disagree. But families are not like civic organizations. There is an organic relationship within families, not a set of rules for membership. There's no bouncer at the door. No usher checking membership credentials. You sit at table together. You tell stories. You listen. You love each other. You forgive each other.

Church families are like that. Except they're more complex. Differences in church families can be greater and relationships often less intimate. But welcoming others in the name of Jesus is nonnegotiable. Reconciliation in our church families is possible. And it's urgent. It's part of our nature and our identity. If there's going to be reconciliation, let it be at the table of our Lord. Let it be with the family.

But that begs the question. Who can be in the family? Who is welcome at the table? Can gays come to the table?

Are the doors to the church-family home open to some but closed to others? Is the Lord's table restricted? Are some barred? If so, who? Who is fenced out? Who is refused? Are the wealthy barred from our table? Jesus said it's almost impossible for rich people to enter the kingdom of God.[9] So, should wealthy people be screened before being allowed to come to the table? Hundreds of passages in Scripture condemn greed. Not in three or four places but in hundreds. There's no ambiguity about it. Should people whose lives and behavior reflect greed be barred from the Lord's table? What about intolerant people, judgmental people, arrogant people? Arrogance, you understand, is called an abomination in Scripture.[10] Do you know any arrogant people in your church? Or what about liars? Should people who lie be barred? Turns out lying is considered an abomination too.[11] But aren't people who lie welcome at our table? We'd have few people in church if we barred liars.

We invite people to the table who gossip even though their gossip can destroy people's lives and tear up a church. We invite divorced people, people who've committed adultery, impatient people, people who quarrel, who are angry, who are jealous, who divide the church, and who are dishonest in their work, another abomination before God.[12] Should they all be allowed to come to the table? Or should we ask some to step outside while the faithful, only those we see as truly righteous, take communion? And then, which group am I in? If things were divvied up at your church, where would you fall—with the ones who are righteous enough to be allowed at the table or with the ones who should be barred because of their sins?

I'm sensing a trend in my conversations with some Christian leaders that opposition not just to gay marriage but even to talking about inclusion of gays at the Lord's table or in any other sort of Christian fellowship is becoming a line in the sand. In other words, we can talk about lots of issues and will be open to differences among churches on many practices, but we will stand firm on this one. Differences of opinion on this issue, even if the conversation is on biblical grounds, will not be considered or tolerated.

There's a long history of lines in the sand among Christians. Some are old and feel quaint, like the line in the sand about the Earth being the center of the universe, though I'm sure Christian believers like Galileo Galilei didn't think this line was all that quaint. In my lifetime, Christian leaders drew a line in the sand against Blacks attending white churches. Less than forty years ago, many congregations drew a line in the sand about allowing divorcees to lead a prayer or teach a class. Lines in the sand have a tendency to shift as the winds blow. Not always, but sometimes, such winds are signs of God's Spirit. But here's the question: Does this drawing of a line, this desire to not even talk about or think about gays in the kingdom, reflect the gospel? Does it lead to life? Is this exclusion of people the glimpse of God that Christians want to exhibit to the world? Is this what Christians should be known for, saying no to even talking about our differences?

Jesus said, I'm not here for the righteous but for the sinners. So, who are these sinners that Jesus keeps eating with? If your answer is, "Well, people, you know, like all those other folks," then you miss Jesus's point. You misunderstand what's at stake in the passage. The answer is, I am. I'm the sinner. You are. Jesus isn't talking about other people, the ones we're uncomfortable with, people we'd rather not think about or hang out with, people we're hurt by or angry at, people who have been unfair to us, people whose politics we find contemptible, people we find repulsive or odd or wrong. He's not looking at them. He's looking at you. He's talking to me. Which one of us is righteous enough, pure enough, or knowledgeable enough to decide who is welcome and who is not?

Whose table is it anyway? Who's responsible for sending out the invitations and deciding who can be given a seat? Or here's a question. Isn't it a little awkward that the host at the table, and I mean the table right there in church, in front of God and everyone, has a reputation for partying it up with sinners? It's tempting to give the Pharisees a high-five on that one—it feels unseemly, inappropriate, it's a bad look, what would people say, and all that. But the host of the banquet says: Hey, I'm throwing a party. He pulls in some of his most devoted followers and tells them: Go out into the streets and lanes of the town and bring the outcasts to my party, the ones no one wants to be with, those who are considered unclean, unacceptable, unwanted. And if the table isn't full yet, then go out beyond the city gates, to society's edge, to people not remotely like you, to ones you couldn't imagine talking to or being with, and urge them to come so that my house may be filled.[13]

We were invited to that party, you and I. We received personal invitations. Which ones of us decided not to come because Jesus had invited some folks we were uncomfortable with or didn't like very much or didn't dress like we do or vote like we do, people who live on the other side of the line in the sand, the line we decided to draw? And which ones of us came and enjoyed the banquet so much that we stayed and stayed and danced the night away?

~

Most of the partygoers are gone now. There's still some food left and a few stragglers. Simon has a chicken leg in his hand, waving it around, making gestures, still telling stories as Andrew and John dodge the drippings. Martha is folding tablecloths and putting the centerpieces away. Across the lawn, some of the latecomers, the ones who live way out in the country, are trying to teach some of the disciples how to line dance. Levi has two left feet, but he's game and is giving it a good effort. You can hear the laughter all the way across the village.

Jesus sits down with a sigh. It was a good party. He loved those who came. His heart still hurt for those who didn't. He pointed to a chair nearby and gestured for one of his disciples to join him. "How was it out there beyond the city roads? Did you have any trouble getting people to come?"

"No, not really. Most of them seemed eager. I loved every minute of it."

"You're good at it," Jesus said. "It made a difference."

They sat quietly for a minute or two. Sometimes it's nice just to be with people you love. But it was getting late. The disciple stood up and smiled. It was time to turn in. "Good night, Lord." Jesus smiled back with his whole face. "Good night, Mattie."

11

ALEXA, ADD JESUS TO THE GROCERY LIST

The people are known for their hospitality. I've never experienced anything quite like it.

It's not that other cultures don't offer words and acts of hospitality. Every place does. In most places I have visited, the people I have met have been generous and warm, gracious and kind. People are good. Most of us are, at least most of the time. Or we want to be. Or we are when we're at our best. I want to think the best about people. I don't want to become cynical. Sometimes people can be hurtful or hard-edged. Sometimes Christians are. More often than I wish, I am. But when people can stop for a minute and listen to one another, when we can sit down together and share lives, our fears and our joys, we can be awfully bighearted, tolerant, forgiving, and kind. Our current polarizations, at least in the States, can make being with people who are not like us daunting or difficult. It doesn't have to be that way. I don't want to give up on people. I want to be better at the gift of welcome.

But I've never known an entire culture where the spirit of welcome is so conspicuous as it is in Ghana, West Africa. I'm not trying to make a competitive statement, like which nation is best at welcoming—we're number one; no, we're number one. I think I could make an argument on behalf of pretty much every country I've visited. People are kind everywhere and are welcoming in different ways. But for the Ghanaian people, a spirit of welcome is stitched into their consciences, their community, and their language. If a Ghanaian does not welcome a stranger well, they can bring shame upon themselves, their family, their people.

The word is *Akwaaba*. You see it everywhere, from the moment you arrive to the moment you leave. You hear it every day. *Akwaaba*: "You are welcome." It's not just a word. It's also a moral understanding, a commitment, a habit, a way of being. It comes from the Akan people, the largest indigenous group in the modern nation of Ghana. *Akwaaba* is not the word used in response to someone's "Thank you." It's not a throwaway line or an afterthought or an act of etiquette—remember, child, to say "Please" and "*Akwaaba*."

It generally begins the conversation: "You are welcome." You are welcome here. Please come into my home. Come to my table. You are my honored guest. Though it can be a little jolting to the ears of English speakers, a Ghanaian greeting often begins with "You are welcome," to which the appropriate response is, "Thank you." A fascinating reversal.

Think that through for a minute. Welcome initiates the conversation. Welcome initiates everything. Nothing in the culture takes place that is not immersed in welcome. Friends are welcome. Strangers are welcome. Enemies are welcome. Guests are welcome. The other is always served first and best. To eat in a Ghanaian home is to be honored profoundly and sacrificially. Ghanaian families may serve a meal to an out-of-country guest equivalent to a week's worth, or a month's worth, of family income. And you can't stop it. They're choosing to do it for you because that's what hospitality demands, because you are genuinely welcome. The only possible response is to say, "Thank you."

Several of us who had recently been together in Ghana were riding in a rental car from Bozeman, Montana, to Yellowstone National Park. The drive is spectacular. The closer we got to the park, the more riveting the beauty became. With the Gallatin Mountain Range now behind us, the road began to narrow, winding its way through the

Yellowstone River valley. Every now and then, we would pull over just to absorb the sheer wonder of it. We would think, now that's the most beautiful thing I've ever seen, then we would round another bend, and a new panorama of splendor would smack us in the face.

As dusk began to descend, we pulled over one last time to see the river, the trees and hills, to soak up the sunset's palette of goldenrod and amber, blush, coral, sienna and saffron, teal, lavender, and indigo, which infused the setting with an almost overpowering depth and warmth, shouting to anyone who would hear the praises of nature's brilliance. We were listening. It was Lesa who finally broke our silence. "I believe God is saying to us, '*Akwaaba*.'" Yes, we all thought. That's it. Then all of us, almost instinctively, said, "Thank you."

Our world is awash in the greatness and power and goodness of God. There are moments, too rare, when we are simply stunned by its beauty. We sense that God may be saying to us and all of creation, "Welcome." And our hearts want to cry out, "Thank You." But most of the time, we are too busy to notice, or the people and activities around us are too familiar, or the weight of our many stresses distracts us to the point that we can't even see the river or hear God's welcome.

It's not that God's glory is always and altogether hidden. The biggest problem is us. We are inclined toward what my old friend Charles Siburt called "self-tacklization." We get in our own way, stumble over our own feet, grab our own facemask and throw ourselves to the ground, and then complain about the penalty. We can be our own worst enemy. Our habits and inattention and disinterest, or our self-centeredness and indignation and complacency, have over time revealed imperfections in our mind's eye, leaving floating shadows that obstruct and imperil our ability to see the working of God in our midst. Or we just poke our eyes out with a stick. But one thing we know about Jesus, he's good at making the blind see. It might take an eye ointment of spittle-and-dirt, but what's a little mud in your eye when the glory of God is at stake?

It feels trite to say that the best way to see God is in the small things. Perhaps it's true, but not because God exists only in small things. It's a question of our eyesight, not God's presence. Humans tend to be drawn to the spectacular. We love the brilliant, the bountiful, the breathtaking. It's hard to miss God's glory at Yellowstone. But seeing God in the small things, the mundane things, requires a measure of discipline to train our watchfulness and our patience.

Seeing God in the little ways is to follow in the path of Brother Lawrence, the seventeenth-century French monk, the former soldier injured in battle, who chose a quiet way to serve God for the rest of his life, who saw himself as no one, nobody, just working quietly, obediently, in the monastery, writing a few notes about the God he encountered while chopping potatoes and scrubbing dishes, or standing before a tree in winter considering the flowering and fruit that would soon come, every day practicing the presence of God.[1]

"Don't grow tired of doing little things for the love of God," Brother Lawrence said. "God doesn't care so much about the size of the work, but instead about the love with which it is performed." He didn't intend to write a book. He just took some notes over the years, which were gathered and published after his death, becoming one of the great devotional classics in the history of Christianity. That would have surprised him. What would also have surprised him is how his spiritual practices have been so hyper-individualized by modern Christians. He was part of a community. He was accountable to others. He didn't always enjoy what he did. But you do things for the sake of God and also for the sake of others.

Here are some ways in which we may be able to discern God—not just in small things, and not only in solitude, but in relationships, coming together with the strangers and friends in our lives, where the hospitality of God may be most visible and most compelling.

~

Alexa, add Jesus to the grocery list. Lesa and I love cooking together. We love the aesthetics of it, the creativity, the ingenuity and imagination. We also love the choreography of it, the rhythm of preparation, the timing, the whisking and stirring, the mixing and pouring, sautéing and stir-frying, the little dance we have to do as one reaches for the refrigerator door while the other suddenly turns to lift a steaming pot off the stove. We normally do the dance well. One of us is light and graceful. Occasionally, however, my big feet interrupt the flow of the whole operation. Or I somehow end up burning my own hand. You mean I need to handle a boiling pot of linguini with a potholder? Ah, but the outcome of our kitchen work is delicious. We do love cooking together.

We don't, however, love wrestling the crowds at the grocery store. People can be crazy in there. I mean bat guano crazy. Some people seem not to be aware that there are other people around them—you know, busy people, pressed for time, need to go, things to do, gotta get the crushed San Marzano tomatoes to make the pasta sauce because we've got church friends coming over tonight, maneuvering the cart through the labyrinth of slow and thoughtless people, like the mom whose child seems to be running through the store without any supervision or the older couple who stand in front of the salad dressings for half the day deciding between the classic ranch and the creamy parmesan ranch as the young woman down the aisle holds up thirty or so irritable shoppers while she texts her boyfriend on her smartphone.

On one of those normal days at the supermarket, Lesa and I were looking over our shopping list on our Amazon Alexa app. Most every day, one or the other of us will tell the smart device in our house what should be added to the grocery list. Since, in our latter years, we can no longer remember things, being able to tell "Alexa" what we need has kept our lives relatively organized. So, Lesa had her phone out. I was looking over her shoulder, skimming through the list. I don't know if we were clogging the aisle or not—they can just wait; those people sure can be impatient. Then we saw the word at about the same time. Down toward the bottom of the list, along with the bacon, sour cream, and lunch meat, was the word "Jesus."

Who put Jesus on the grocery list? We're not sure. Well, we—and when I say we, I mean I—think possibly Lesa, who has the most adorable Texas accent, might have told Alexa to add "cheeses" to the grocery list, except Alexa apparently is not fluent in Texan, so Jesus was added instead. We had a good laugh. But then, what do we do now that Jesus is on our grocery list? Turns out it was strangely re-centering. Now that we were aware that Jesus was with us, we felt some pressure to, I don't know, possibly act like Jesus would act.

With Jesus on our grocery list, we found ourselves a little kinder. We stepped back and let the older couple make their bold salad dressing choice—it was the parmesan—without my needing to drop a heavy sigh just loud enough for them to hear. We smiled and nodded to the mother with the small child, who was well aware of how difficult it was for the others in the store but wasn't sure if anyone in the store knew how difficult it was for her. We waited as others pushed their way through the carts and shoppers to get a packet of hamburger meat or shredded cheese.

I remembered a comment one of my Black brothers told me once about his grocery store experiences. Watch sometime, he told me, how many Blacks and other persons of color defer to white people in a grocery store. Not always, but noticeably. I know I can sometimes cut through a group of shoppers, reaching in, grabbing my item, and then moving to the next. In my mind, I'm trying to be helpful, acting decisively so that I can get out of the way. But now, it was hard to watch the little dance at the shelves, as some moved in with authority, unawareness, and a sense of entitlement while others stepped back, out of their way. My friend was right. With Jesus now on our grocery list, I had to reconceive the whole thing.

But, of course, Jesus had always been in the aisles with us. I just hadn't noticed. Seeing God in the small things means seeing people, demonstrating understanding rather than aggravation, showing patience, expressing kindness, offering a smile, stepping back, deferring. Seeing God in the small moments is not just appreciating God's presence in the details or the beauty of our world or the ways all the pieces of God's universe seem to dance together for God's glory. It's about seeing the God who has come near, the God with us and within us. It's about the God in the supermarket who sidles up next to you near the heirloom tomatoes and the avocados, whispering, "*Akwaaba*. I see you are here. You are welcome."

God winks on the just and the unjust. Sometimes Christians think that God's blessings go primarily or exclusively to good people. As if blessings are a reward for our salutary behavior or a result of our compelling faith.

I spent a weekend as a young pastor doing a workshop for a congregation in another city. They were delightful people, good and generous folks. They were also quite wealthy. I hadn't picked up on that before the weekend. It wasn't so much the rich part that disturbed me, though I'm certainly aware of how spiritually perilous wealth can be. It was the fact that they believed their wealth was the result of a promise from God, tied to their faith. I began to hear it in comments and conversations, then more overtly in the Sunday worship. If you have faith, God will bless you. If you have not been financially successful, then you must not have faith.

The sheer logic of the argument has never made a lot of sense to me. If God favors the good people and disfavors the not-so-good, then the math of that quid pro quo would, at some point, skew the blessings toward all the good people. If doing the right thing makes a person healthy, wealthy, and wise, why would anyone choose differently? Of course, the world doesn't work like that. Evil people often succeed, and faithful people often catch it in the neck. So what is God doing? And how do I get in line for my blessings?

In the Sermon on the Mount, Jesus said to the crowd, "Your Father in heaven . . . makes his sun rise on the evil and on the good and sends rain on the righteous and on the unrighteous."[2] The same sun that shines on the honest farmer's land also shines on the deceitful farmer's land. And the rain falls on both fields just the same. God smiles on both. You can't tell by looking at the harvest which one the Father has blessed. No one is advantaged or disadvantaged in that way.

So, why did Jesus insert this point into his sermon? What was he getting at? The preceding verses may help: "You have heard that it was said, 'You shall love your neighbor and hate your enemy.' But I say to you, 'Love your enemies and pray for those who persecute you.'" In other words, act like God acts. Don't show partiality. Don't just favor the people you like and shun the ones you don't. Love everyone, even those who don't deserve it. That's what God does.

God is sending a downpour of blessings. There's enough rain and sunshine for everyone. But having wealth is not the blessing. In fact, the poor have spiritual advantages over the wealthy. Stop and listen to the Song of Mary sometime, the song sung by Jesus's mother when she met with old Elizabeth. One stanza of her song goes like this:

> He has brought down the powerful from their thrones
> and lifted up the lowly;
> he has filled the hungry with good things
> and sent the rich away empty.[3]

In God's economy, the poor have the advantage. Wealth is not the blessing. The language is even clearer in Luke's version of Jesus's sermon, what we sometimes call the Sermon on the Plain: "Blessed are you who are poor," Jesus said. Not poor in spirit. Just poor. "For yours is the kingdom of God." And then, "Blessed are you who are hungry now, for you will be filled." And "Blessed are you who weep now, for you will laugh."[4] It's a back-to-front, wrong-side-out, up-is-down, rich-is-poor sort of kingdom.

During my years partnering with low-income neighborhoods, a lot of my wealthier friends found the whole thing disconcerting. Why are you down there wasting your time? some would say. This is their own fault. Why don't they just work harder? In other words, *we* are the ones whom God has blessed. Our nice homes and clothes and lifestyles display God's favor.

I've started to avoid phrases like "economically disadvantaged" because in the kingdom of God the poor are rich and the rich are poor. Some things, I think, keep a person from seeing the blessing. Some assets keep us from seeing God. In that way, the wealthy are disadvantaged. One thing was clear to me in those years: My impoverished friends seemed to live with more gratitude, more awareness of God, than those of us who were surrounded by wealth.

How do you know when you've been blessed? It's not like you can measure a blessing. Despite the old song, you can't really count blessings. You don't always recognize the blessing in the moment. Sometimes, what we think are blessings can be curses. The hungry will likely be the most satisfied and the rich the most impoverished, so you can't check your bank account, your refrigerator shelves, or your resume. You may or may not be in good health. You may or may not have the house you want or the job or the spouse or the future you dreamed of.

But you can be kind. People don't have to know what you've said or done. Their praise of you isn't necessary. Just be kind, every day, in small ways. You can love people who cross you or gossip about you or hurt you or ignore you. It won't be easy, but you can love them. Love your enemies, Jesus said. God winks on the just and the unjust, the good and the bad. God rains on the crazy and the not quite as crazy, the easy to be with and some pretty tough old birds, and so can you. Love those who persecute you or demean you or challenge you. You can love them, even if they don't love you back, even if they don't say they're sorry. Apologizing, of course, is a good thing. It's certainly the right thing for the one who wounded you. But it's not a prerequisite for your compassion or your forgiveness. Your job is not to fold your arms and turn your face away until they apologize. And cling to your grudge when they finally do. Your job is to love them.

And here's the miracle. Here is God's gift. At some point, it won't matter whether or not they love you back. It won't matter whether you got everything in life you wanted. That's not the blessing anyway. The blessing is the gift of seeing others as God sees you.

~

When grace slaps you in the face, turn the other cheek. "Community activist" was not a title I ever sought or felt comfortable with. There was a time, sadly, when it had some negative political connotations for some folks. But I began to grow more comfortable with it in retrospect, long after I moved away from that city and that work.

I think many people think of an activist as someone who stirs something up or stirs people up, perhaps causing a riot or lighting a car on fire. That's not what I was, of course. I've begun to wonder what the alternative is to being an activist. If I'm not active in a cause, then I'm passive or perhaps ignorant. If I'm not activating—that is, initiating, energizing, and empowering, or at least involved, engaged, and participating—then I'm basically sitting back and watching.

There's a concept in mass communication studies, popularized in the early days of television, called "narcotizing dysfunction."[5] The theory is that the more inundated people are by media, the more apathetic they become. They're numbed and nonfunctioning. They watch TV—and in this day and age, engage in social media in all its forms and addictions—and begin to think: I know some things, I have some ideas, I can make some arguments, therefore I must be doing something. But all they're doing is sitting on a couch watching television. Or they're glued to a keyboard and screen. Their consciences are clear because they're more informed, or believe they are. But they're not engaged. They're not actually doing anything.

I was forced to do something. It was uncomfortable at first, but it was my job. I had to step up. The deeper into it I got, the clearer it became that I had, up to that point, known nothing, really. Reading some articles and watching the news had kept me on the sidelines. Now I had been tossed into the deep end of the pool.

My first work was to direct and teach a college-level course in the humanities to adult students living below the poverty line. We provided food for each class because many of the students would not have eaten that day. We provided transportation to those who needed it so they could get to the classroom—the local Uber office agreed to provide free rides to the students who needed it. The sight of a limousine dropping off one of our students made all of us smile.

There were almost thirty students in the first cohort, studying English, philosophy, the arts, history, and critical thinking. I shared the teaching with four other faculty. My area was critical thinking. I had taught a lot of college students before, but none as hungry, in every sense of the word, as these students. All but about three in the first class had done prison time. Most had lived very hard lives. My world and theirs hardly overlapped. There were times I felt totally lost, dazed, like I had been slapped in the face by God's grace. I never doubted that the work was a gift from God, but it was the hardest thing I had ever done.

A couple of nights before the English faculty member was to begin his part of the course, he had to drop out. It was last minute, and we couldn't find another teacher, so as the director of the program I had to step in. The topic areas in the syllabus were Langston Hughes, the Harlem Renaissance, and spoken word poetry, including poetry slam and def jam. I knew how foolish it was going to be for the white guy to lead this discussion. I crammed like crazy. When the class began, the students were silent. It was simply miserable. They were disappointed because the professor they were anticipating wasn't there. But it also felt awkward, inauthentic, for me to be teaching them something they knew more about than I did.

Then the laughter came, first from a couple of the women who watched me struggle with the words and the rhythm of one of the def jam poems. And then I laughed. And then the whole room. Then came the onslaught of jibes and friendly insults, to me and one another. They became the teachers. I became the student. I slipped in a little history they didn't know. They taught me the inferences in the language I was totally missing. Something changed that night, in them and in me. I allowed myself to be immersed in a culture I was not part of, to feel embarrassed, even a little humiliated. I gave up what dignity I had. But I was all in. And they welcomed me. They gave me themselves. In time, they shared stories they had never shared before to a person like me, a white professor, an outsider, the man. It was one of the greatest gifts of grace I had ever received.

Here's what I learned. If you're slapped in the face by grace, turn the other cheek and ask for more. If you're hit hard with a circumstance you would never have chosen, by an obstacle that seems insurmountable, walk in, embrace it, and wait for more grace. I know a thousand exceptions to that charge. You do too. I'm not talking about accepting abuse. I'm not suggesting a sort of spiritual masochism, where you receive or impart injury upon yourself or anyone else. I'm suggesting, rather, that life circumstances aren't always predictable and that often the greatest blessings are the most difficult.

We deprive ourselves of some of God's greatest gifts because we prefer to be comfortable, to be in situations we already know. It's easier to sit on the couch in front of the TV than it is to be among people who are different from you. Get up. Put your phone in your pocket. Shut off your social media feeds for a minute. Get out past the fortress of the familiar. Become active in a cause greater than you. If you're wondering where God is or what God is telling you or where God is calling you, you will see God in new ways, but it will be outside the citadels of your church or your neighborhood.

Be prepared to be awkward, self-conscious, unsettled, unnerved. You'll be an outsider, but that's a good thing. Jesus was an outsider. He knows a thing or two about that. The earliest Christians were outsiders. That's part of the deal. But don't wait for God to tell you to go. God isn't sitting on a throne somewhere in the part of town you live in, pointing a long, bony finger out toward the hinterlands, telling you in somber tones, "Go into all the world." God is already there, among those you are most uncomfortable with, the ones you struggle to be with or like.

God isn't waiting on you. God's work began out there a long time ago. God is aware of you. God knows who you are, what you can do and what you can't, what you can bear and what you shouldn't. God puts the rake down, takes a sip of water, wipes the perspiration away, and says to you, "Put some work clothes on. I need you here."

~

Church Actually. Every church member is an expert. At least most are. Or believe they are. Most have a good sense as to what church ought to be like, how worship should go, what songs are best, how sermons should be preached, how decisions should be made. That's not terribly surprising. We all come with a history. Most of us have seen other churches in other places. Or we've had enough experiences away from a body of believers to know what's helpful and what's just religious gimcrackery. We know what we like and what we don't. Most of us aren't complainers. Well, we may complain a little to our family or friends, but we're not going to make a big scene. We're not going to walk away in a huff if things don't go our way. Not most of the time. But that doesn't mean we're not still evaluating, still measuring things against the standard embedded in our minds.

The days are long past since Christians were organized in neighborhood parishes, when we accepted whatever priest or pastor we were given, when there was nowhere else to go. Today we have choices. Lots of choices. Our culture is steeped in choices. We can choose to be a part of a church or not. We can go to this one or, if we're unhappy with it, move to that one. We can find just the right mix of formal and casual, liturgical or free, high church or low, electric guitar or pipe organ. If we don't like it, we can complain. I don't know the songs anymore. I don't know what the preacher was talking about. We got out awfully late. And in the midst of all the noise—the disinterest, dissatisfaction, and disapproval—too many of us are going away hungry. We aren't being spiritually nourished. We aren't being filled.

I wish I were exempt from the small-mindedness of it all. I have served as a pastor and know what it's like to feel criticized. Any church I'm part of, or even visit, I am consciously an advocate of the pastor and staff. I want them to feel supported and encouraged. But I have sometimes let my guard down with lay members. In congregations where non-clergy can play large roles in the worship service as well as leadership in the church's ministries, I have sometimes, embarrassingly, found myself more critical of church members than I should be.

A well-meaning young man walked to the table and began his communion meditation: "Well, on my way to church this mornin' I drove past my favorite doughnut and coffee shop, and it reminded me of our Lord's Supper . . ." My heart sank. I was pretty sure there was no way to recover from that, though apparently some in the congregation enjoyed the doughnut shout-out.

But the problem in this tale is not them. Let's be clear about that. The problem is the inner critic that has taken up residence in my own heart, the one I've been trying to get rid of for years. He won't go away. Just keeps coming back. I tied him to a stake once and lit a fire at his feet. The fire petered out. He told me the problem was that I hadn't laid the wood down correctly and should have doused it with kerosene first. The little critic won't die.

A turning point took place for me several years ago when I was visiting a church in another city. A Lord's Supper meditation was particularly painful. I said nothing, but I was pretty worked up. This is not what the Lord's Supper means, I thought. It's not what it's for. Teaching like that will malform a church body. Later that day, I shared my concern with another minister, a person I knew well and trusted. He asked me a simple question: "Have you never preached a sermon you were later embarrassed about?" I began to review in my mind some of the sermons I had preached and classes I had taught. Some of the memories made me cringe. Some made me want to throw up. Some were truly awful. Some were, frankly, dangerous. But you know, I had given myself a whole lot of grace over the years. I had given myself room to grow. Why couldn't I do that with fellow Christ followers?

The genius of the church is that it's made up of humans. Christ was enfleshed in an ordinary human body. He didn't shame it or replace it or build a fire under it and douse it with kerosene. He loved it and redeemed it. The church is filled with ordinary, fallible, not-sure-what-to-do, messed up, misunderstanding, misspoken, mistaken men and women. Christ took this ordinary body of disciples and transformed it. What was plain, imperfect, blind, sometimes inept, and often sinful, God made holy. And my nature, my job, my calling was to, what, critique these people? Repudiate them? Keep them away from a microphone? Send their children home in sackcloth and ashes? Who do I think I am? What gives me the right to judge a person for whom Christ died, as though I were standing at Christ's side sending sheep one way and goats another?

Ron Rolheiser has said it well: "You cannot deal with a perfect, all-loving, all-forgiving, all-understanding God in heaven, if you cannot deal with a less-than-perfect, less-than-forgiving, and less-than-understanding community here on earth. You cannot pretend to be dealing with an invisible God if you refuse to deal with a visible family."[6]

Father Rolheiser's call is not for us to simply be more tolerant or less critical. That's a hard lesson, but most people can learn that in a weekend seminar. It is to embrace the deeply flawed people in the church as the sanctified body of Christ, fit for the work to which God has called them. When they speak, when they pray, when they break bread, when they sing, when they serve, Christ is incarnate again. In spite of our inadequacies, Christ has come and made his home here, not just among us but in us.

~

It was a long day. I was still tired from my long flight to Accra. I had been up early, eating breakfast with Samuel, my host and the headmaster at the school where I was to teach. Theresa had made an American breakfast. I had asked—I always asked, with a smile on my face—for traditional Ghanaian fufu, a ground meal made from cassava, plantains, and cocoyam and then boiled and pounded, knowing I would be denied. Samuel, my host and friend, was watching out for me. Ghanaian hospitality only goes so far. He would not allow me to be sick. After the delicious eggs, we made our way across the city, where the university students were waiting.

I climbed out of the van and reached for my backpack. A student jumped in ahead of me and grabbed it. I told him it was just my bag with books and teaching notes and that I could carry it. "No," he said, "it is my honor to carry it for you every day during this course. *Akwaaba*." I stopped and smiled. "Thank you."

After a long day of teaching and conversation, I joined the family in Samuel and Theresa's living room. Their children shared stories about their day. The evening meal was almost ready. Samuel turned to me. "How was your day?" he asked. It had been a good day. The students worked hard. I told him how odd it felt not to be able to carry my own bag, but how hard the students had worked to serve and honor their guest, this stranger in their midst.

"Of course," Samuel said. "But you are not a stranger. This is your home. You are welcome."

12

WHEN CERTAINTY IS FRACTURED

I was both excited and exhausted, worn out from my morning responsibilities but looking forward to what would happen later that day. I was a young senior pastor at a growing church. I had preached at two services that morning, taught a class, greeted members in the foyer—some who loved my sermon, one or two not so much—wrestled the kids into the car to get a quick bite at a nearby restaurant, hoping to have a little nap time before my 3:00 appointment, the one I had made with myself. There was an important football game on, and nothing could keep me from watching it.

It was Dallas against Washington, perennial powerhouse teams. I had followed the Cowboys since the franchise began in 1960. I had wept over their devastating loss to the Packers in the 1967 "Ice Bowl." I was glued to the set at all five Super Bowl appearances in the 1970s. I knew for certain that the Cowboys would be vying for the championship every year. It's 1983. Can you imagine Dallas not making the playoffs? Washington, on the other hand, was the hated enemy, our rival, the team that always contended against the Cowboys for the championship. That would never change. The season was almost over. Every game counted. The conference championship was on the line.

The teams came onto the field. The Dallas home crowd was roaring. Trumpet player Tommy Loy walked to the fifty-yard line and played the National Anthem, a single instrument, clear, confident, and compelling. I had goosebumps. I sat on the edge of the couch, ready for the kickoff. And the phone rang.

Who could possibly be calling at such a time? I considered letting the call go. But I felt like I had to answer it. It might be someone from the church. I had responsibilities. And surely the call wouldn't last long. It didn't. But when I hung up, which team won this or any other game meant nothing to me. Absolutely nothing. Things change. Predictability is not a hard science. Certainty is almost never certain. You just never know.

The caller was a friend. Had I heard, he asked, that one of our members, his name was Joe, had accidentally backed his car over his young son? You better get to the hospital, he said. I don't know if his boy will make it.

I was less than ten minutes away. I jumped in the car and raced through the neighborhood, my mind playing out various scenarios. They would be counting on me. I was a young pastor. I wasn't very experienced at this sort of thing, but I needed to step up. What should I say? As I pulled into the hospital parking lot, I had finalized my plan. If the son, Joey, were alive, I would talk to them about hope, about strength in times of trouble. A psalm or two had come to mind. I could use the words of those psalms. But then it hit me. I had forgotten my Bible. In my rush to get to the hospital, I had left my Bible at the house. What kind of pastor was I? Maybe I could paraphrase a psalm or two. And I would pray with them, of course. But if Joey had not made it, well, I wasn't exactly sure. This was new ground for me. What do you say to a family whose three-year-old child was dead? I trusted that the words would come. I was good with words. Surely, I would know what to say.

I walked into the waiting room. A half dozen folks had already arrived. I looked at their faces. I didn't have to ask what Joey's condition was. He was gone. He was three years old, and he was gone. One of them led me to the room. I knocked softly and opened the door. Joe jumped from his seat, grabbed me by my arm, and said, "I need to walk." I nodded. I had still said nothing. I was trying to play the role of a pastor, even if I didn't know exactly what I was doing. My plan had been to give him a hug and say something, surely something, but he was pushing me toward the door before I could do anything. I found myself juggling my grief and my responsibilities and felt like I was failing at both.

We navigated through some cars that were dropping patients and family members off, walked a few more yards, and then Joe crumpled onto the hospital lawn, sobbing. All I could do was sit on the grass, hold him, and cry. I kept thinking, I've got to be strong. I have to say something. I need to know what to say. But I didn't. I had no idea. People walked by us on their way to the hospital entrance, staring. I didn't want Joe to see that. I pulled his head to my shoulder. His grip on my forearm was so tight I could no longer feel my fingers. I don't know how long we were there.

After a while, Joe sat back, silently, just staring at the lawn, which only weeks before had been a deep, luscious green but was now yellowed and dry because winter had set in. Spring was a long way off. It might not ever come. I sat with him and waited. I don't think I have ever seen such despair. My heart was crushed. He finally looked up into my eyes, reached toward my face, held it in his hands, and asked me, "Will I ever laugh again?"

What were the right words to respond to that question? I struggled. I hesitated. I ended up saying nothing. What would you say at that point? How about something like, "Sure you will, Joe. God will take care of you. You will find joy again." But I couldn't say it. It would have sounded flip. Hollow. Even cruel. Truth be told, I simply wasn't sure. I wasn't sure what God was doing. I wasn't sure God was doing anything. I had no idea how this could have happened or why. I certainly didn't have a lot of answers for Joe that day.

It's easy to talk about faith in God on paper, faith as an abstraction. It's easy to say you can know that God is with you, that God is in charge of the universe, and that everything is going to be okay. But everything isn't always okay. This was not okay. Joe and Kay had two bright, wonderful daughters and a sweet, good son. Children come to families with hope glued to their hearts. They bring with them a sense of promise. Of life. Of a future. You know you can't predict everything that will happen, but you see the days ahead, teaching your boy to ride a bike just as you had done with his sisters, holding his hand on his first day of school, standing to scream and holler as he walks across the graduation stage attired in his cap, tassel, and gown. But now, those days would never come. And it's not okay.

Wouldn't it be appropriate to wonder about the working of God in the wake of such a tragedy? To at least ask questions about what kind of world God had made that would allow such anguish? What can we count on when all is said and done? Will the rug always be pulled out from under us? Is God responsible for this? How long, Lord, will your face be turned from me?

These are hard questions, but they aren't the sorts of questions that undercut faith. On the contrary, they stretch our faith and expand faith's imagination. They energize it and enrich it. Or at least they can. The alternative—saying nothing, asking nothing, doubting nothing—while it seems easier, less bothersome, less conflictual, has its own downside. Avoiding the hard questions may seem to be the more faithful walk with God, but the questions come anyway, unbidden, unwelcome, and often in circumstances when they can't be sufficiently dealt with. Avoiding the hard questions often delays and ultimately amplifies the crisis when it comes. Avoiding the hard questions about God, in all frankness, has a greater likelihood of leading to the total rejection of God than living with the questions all along.

I hear from time to time about some Christian leaders who say that doubting God is dangerous, even sinful. Words fail me. Have they not known loss? Have they never questioned God? Have they never said in their hearts, I just don't know? Have they never read the Psalms? What kind of faith prohibits the hard questions? A timid faith? A fearful faith? A faithless faith? Is a faith that avoids the doubts hefty enough, malleable enough, demanding enough to face the troubles? For surely troubles will come. And when they do, don't be surprised when our certainty is fractured, when the external props that have held our faith up are too brittle to carry the weight, and the whole structure crumbles.

The question that pushed my heart on that hospital lawn, the question that lay unasked for weeks, the one that drove our conversations when the pain lessened and the questions increased, is the question that could not have been and should not have been asked in those first moments of despair. But at some point, it has to be asked. Will you, not knowing all the answers . . . will you, not seeing the outcome . . . will you, while struggling with the doubts like someone who opened a Pandora's box of unanswered or unanswerable questions and is now unable to cram the doubts back in . . . will you, in your uncertainty, trust God anyway?

That's the first question we have to answer. It's the one we began with here and must end with, the hardest question, the trust question: I don't know for sure; yet I will trust. You have to be broke to get there. Simply being broken is not enough. Everyone is broken. Not everyone allows themselves to be broke. But there's a second question that must also be asked, no less important but asked too seldom. Yes, I will trust, but what difference will it make? What behavior will it change? What life will it touch? I will trust, but what will I do then?

~

I put the T-shirt that the paramedic had given me, the one with the double-helix strands shaped into the image of a cross, into my closet beside all the other shirts—a Nike shirt, an Adidas shirt (just maintaining bipartisanship), a Reese's Peanut Butter Cups shirt, a couple of Iowa Hawkeye jerseys, and a shirt with the slogan "I Walked the Wall," indicating that I had completed, when I was much younger, the eighty-four-mile trek along Hadrian's Wall in England from the North Sea to the Irish Sea. I mostly forgot about the DNA-cross shirt. I wasn't avoiding wearing it. It now has an honored place in my wardrobe. I just wasn't wearing any of my T-shirts, not because it was too cold—it was mid-summer in sultry South Texas—but because I was tired, deeply fatigued, and mostly in bed.

After my stroke scare, I checked out of the hospital not knowing the answers to most of my questions. I knew a few things. I knew, after two days of tests, that there had been no discernable damage to my brain or my heart. I knew that hospital food without salt or fat was utterly tasteless. I knew that I loved Lesa more than ever after she slipped me a pepperoni pizza on the second night. I ate it quickly, worried that the nurses might take it away, but when I was discovered, they mostly just expressed jealousy as the aroma of fresh pizza wafted down the hospital corridors. I knew I was still having spells of lightheadedness. I almost blacked out while walking with the nurse on my way out of the hospital. They hadn't been able to find a wheelchair. They had asked if I was okay to walk. Sure, I said. Absolutely. No problem. I got this. I made it about ten steps toward the elevator before the hallway started spinning out of control. In a matter of seconds, a wheelchair was found. What I still didn't know was what caused the episode in the first place.

It would be months before I could get in to see the neurologist and the cardiologist. Until then, I was committed to doing everything I could to get well. What I imagined was a few weeks of taking long walks, talking often with our church's ministers where I had served on staff, catching up on some reading, and finding some new dinner recipes. That was foolish. What I mostly did was lie in bed. I don't mean I was dishonest in bed, you understand, just prostrate. All this was new for me. I had been healthy all my life. Now I was too tired to walk to the front door.

Beside me in the bed every day were my dogs and my computer. The puppies were thrilled with this new development. They snored next to my leg most of each day. As for the computer, there was this book about faith and doubt I had been wanting to write. I pounded on the keyboard between naps—some days a few hours, some days a few minutes. I was able to get out some, have a meal with friends, go to church most Sundays, but I stayed mostly in or near my bed. That was eight months ago as of this writing. They have been days of clarity.

The book I had in mind was not merely a writing project. It was personal. I had lived with questions about my faith and my doubts much of my adult life. I needed to sort through some things, ask some questions, examine my heart, and pray. As much as anything, I needed to slow down. I had been busy, too busy, for a very long time, including four good but unexpected years as executive minister at my church. I thought I was getting the hectic pace of my life under control by announcing my retirement, scheduled for the end of June. But the EMS workers were in my bedroom a month before that. I decided I'd better pay attention. So I propped myself up in bed each morning, told "Alexa" to play Brandi Carlile on my smart speaker, and began to write.

I knew I wanted the title of the book to be *Grace, Sideways*. I had thought about the sideways part for a long time. I had just never experienced God head-on as some of my friends seemed to do. For me, it was always unexpected and a little vague, lingering but opaque. Like a vapor trail. Like a memory.

I struggled for days about whether there should be a comma between "Grace" and "Sideways." I kept thinking of a story I had heard years ago about some famous author, perhaps Oscar Wilde, who was asked at the end of the day, "How did your writing go," to which he supposedly replied something like, "I spent the first half of the day deciding to take a comma out and the second half of the day deciding to put it back in." I always felt that story was bogus or at least an exaggeration. But then I found myself spending days paralyzed about the comma. Was it necessary? Was it superfluous? And then, on another goose chase about a different matter, I found an article by an art critic about the Japanese word *ma*, that empty space so crucial to Japanese art and design. And I thought, that's exactly what this comma is. The comma was the *ma*, not just in the title but in the whole story. The comma had to stay.

But then the larger truth began to emerge. After years—come to think of it, after decades—of too much busyness, too much intensity, too much drivenness, I had stopped. I wish I had chosen it. I wanted to choose it. I knew I needed to choose it. But I finally stopped when I was forced to stop. I hadn't carved out the time, but a time was carved out for me when I could reimagine my life and my faith. I was living in my own *ma*, a time of emptiness that wasn't truly empty, of space, of silence, that had purpose and impact. I was too tired to be driven. I had to rest. But in the rest, new ideas, new imagination, a new vision began to emerge. My stroke scare pushed me off-center, but my off-centeredness brought new beauty. More importantly, I was pushed to think differently. My time and my rest gave me a new perspective. From off-center, I had a better angle to see what was coming at me sideways.

And if *ma* made an interesting metaphor for a comma and for rest, isn't that what doubt is? Don't doubts provide room and perspective? Don't they push faith forward? Aren't they like empty spaces in a painting or a design, not just present but essential? And so, what are my doubts for? What have my doubts done? What have I learned?

Now the issue was not about a comma or even about doubts and certainly not about a book but about my own wrestlings with faith. I was not writing on a subject matter anymore but was on a quest. I had no office to go to, no task to be completed, no lesson to plan, no class to teach, no counsel to offer. I couldn't go anywhere. It was just me on a bed with two snoring King Charles Cavalier Spaniels and my laptop. And a wife, whom I adore, who would come home in the afternoon and ask, "How was your day?" It turned out that my day, each day, was full—typing and thinking and reading and typing some more between multiple naps. I had less energy but more life. I was—oh wait, I remember now all the months I spent reading C. S. Lewis years ago—I was being "surprised by joy." Every day, rest, discovery, renewal, and joy.

So, did God cause this? I had to think about that. I couldn't avoid it. I couldn't run from it. I was writing a book about seeing God, having faith in God. I had to deal with it straight on. The hospital doctors told me I had had a transient ischemic attack, a TIA. So, did God cause my TIA, resulting in my arm and face going numb in the middle of the night? I've thought about it a lot. My answer is still, I don't know. I'm not willing to claim that I'm wiser than I am.

But that's a different question than whether God was present, whether God was at work. I believe God was with me that night. I glimpsed God in the work of the paramedics. I glimpsed God in the prayers of family and friends and church members. God's presence in the minds and hearts of all these people praying brought a lot of folks together on a common journey of faith. What that did in all these lives, only God knows.

As we've seen, the glory of God works in strange ways. Two believers, on their way home to the little village of Emmaus, were walking with a person they didn't know or at least didn't recognize. Was God present with them anyway, even though they didn't see him at first? Is God's glory at play even when the fireworks don't go off, when there are no goosebumps or tears? Or a different question: Would God have been at work even if I hadn't survived the night? My answer to that is yes. I may have doubts, but I've bet my life on that one.

Glimpses of God? Sure. After I went through several weeks of tests, it was finally determined I had blockage in my left anterior descending artery. I would have to have a heart cath, a tube inserted into an artery at my wrist and pushed up into my heart. On the morning of the surgery—early, early in the morning—several friends came to offer support and to be with Lesa during the surgery. Among them were James and Vernita, new friends who were part of our racial healing group. James stood at the foot of my bed, put his hand on my legs, and prayed a moving prayer over me. I saw God in that.

The surgery was successful. They found an 80 percent blockage. A stent was inserted into my artery, opening up the blood flow. The cardiologist said the blockage was not the cause of my TIA or any of my other symptoms. However, fixing it would prevent the stroke I would have had a few years from now. Without the TIA and all the subsequent tests, we wouldn't have known. I saw God in that. The cardiologist told me that other tests had shown I had an atrioventricular (AV) block, a disorder in the electrical impulses in my heart. It was getting worse. It had to be fixed. I needed a pacemaker placed in my chest with leads connected to my heart. If that was successful, it should address all my symptoms. That surgery was done a month later. I saw God in that.

During those weeks, the new executive minister moved to town and brought new life to the work I had been doing. The church seemed to be thriving in my absence. Friends came over and sang with us, ate with us, and laughed with us. Several of our neighbors prepared food and brought it to our house and have continued to pray for us and encourage us. A church member who had cancer, whose immune system was so fragile that she had to avoid contact with almost everyone, sent a gracious card and her prayers. I hadn't remembered to write her, but she had remembered to write me. My strength began to return. Lesa and I could walk the dogs together, walk the grocery store aisles together, and cook together again. I am now back to full health and strength. I have my energy back, my future back. In all these ways, I think God was present. And I'm grateful.

Back at the beginning, I said that I don't normally discern God's grace head-on, that grace doesn't typically grab me by my face and make me look. What can I say? This time it did. I had been looking over to the side, trying to get a glimpse of God out of my peripheral vision. I thought I might see if I could beat the system. A sense of God's presence has almost always come at me sideways, so I was looking for God over there. But, as C. S. Lewis said slyly, God can be very unscrupulous. I had my defense set. I anticipated the other team's moves. I knew the tendencies—how often they ran, how often they passed, when they called a screen or a post or a trap or a draw. I was ready. But God called a misdirection play, the old fumblerooski. I looked left, and grace hit me, full speed, from straight ahead, right at my heart. I see it, Lord. I see.

I've been inundated by signposts these last few months. Everything that has happened has been a blessing, even the hard parts, even the scary parts. These glimpses of God have been both unexpected and welcome. Encountering a signpost is a good thing. It's valuable but only as a pointer to something else, something more.

~

The months after Joey's death were immensely difficult. Joe and Kay visited with Christians who had gone through similar tragedies. There were hard days and nights, hard conversations with their girls, hard decisions to make, hard questions to ask. One development made their lives particularly complex. Shortly before Joey's death, Joe and Kay discovered that they were expecting another child. One would think that such a turn of events might be a blessing when the tragedy occurred. Perhaps in the coming days it could even be a distraction from the heaviness of their grief. But it could also be confusing and painful. This unexpected baby was not and could never be thought of as a replacement for Joey. Joey would have had a baby brother had he lived. They would have grown up together. But that, too, was lost. It was hard not to miss Joey even more now. In the midst of the pregnancy, would they have the time to grieve? Would they be able to find a new rhythm, a new way of being in the world?

Healing was slow. In some ways, healing was never complete. It never is. Wounds can mend, but scars remain. Still, over the months, the family's faith grew. They were surrounded by friends. They became more involved in their community of faith. There was growing light in their eyes.

I remembered—I will never forget—Joe's question on the hospital lawn, "Will I ever laugh again?" In the months after the tragedy, I began to see a measure of joy in Joe's life, but the shadow always seemed to be there. I understood it. The shadow of Joey's death, in a different way and to a lesser degree, lived in my heart, too.

Then, months after Joey died, Kay gave birth to a healthy, sweet baby boy. They named him John, which means "God is merciful." We were elated at the news. I heard through the grapevine that they were bringing the baby to church the following Sunday. He would be a week old.

I met them that morning and hugged them and told them I would say a few things when I got up to preach. I just wanted to fuss over them a little. And so, after the songs, a reading, and a prayer, I walked up on the stage and began to call attention to the baby and the family. But before I could even finish the first sentence, Joe stood and began making his way to the stage, his days-old baby in his arms. My anxiety meter jumped a bit. This is not what I had planned. What would he say? Would it be okay? Would it be helpful to the congregation? More importantly, would it be helpful to Joe and the family?

He reached the stage, walked to the pulpit, and stood for a moment looking at his church family. A smile began to break over his face. And then, seemingly on impulse, he lifted the baby high over his head and held him there for the church to see. He announced with a strong, bold, proud voice, "This is my boy."

It felt like the earth split open. Any sense of Sunday morning normalcy was shattered. It was like, I don't know, it was like God's own heart broke open, and tears of God's grace began to wash over this family, over these people—for our grief, our healing, our rising, our hope. We jumped to our feet, shouting, weeping. I wasn't sure I could breathe. Then, deep from Joe's belly, welling up in his chest, bursting from his throat, shaking the room, came the sound of full-on, extravagant, joy-filled, heart-wrenching, life-giving laughter.

God's grace grasps us without warning. We don't see it coming. We're not sure we believe it at first. We may not even recognize it. And, truth be told, we don't always know for sure. But having doubts doesn't mean your faith has failed. It means you're still showing up, paying attention, on your toes, seeking God, letting go. Anyone can believe when the sun's out and the answers come easy. The question is, can you trust God at nightfall when all you've got is a "maybe" or an "I don't know." Or in the quiet when your prayers are whispered, unsteady, unsure. Or on the hospital lawn, on yellowed grass, in the winter, through the tears, when spring is little more than a wish or a memory. Here, between the hope and the uncertainty, is where faith finds its courage.

Pain, disappointment, and grief are signs that we are still alive—emerging, changing, perhaps flourishing, even when we let others down, even when we're confused or distraught, even when we're too ashamed to look God in the eye and confess the truth about ourselves. Faith doesn't depend on our excellence at faith-making. Rather, faith ripens, lengthens, sweetens, softens, wizens as God, beyond all comprehension, begins to nourish in our hearts new life. Then hope will rise with the sun. Then laughter will awaken the dead. Then, at last, we will see the way home.

ACKNOWLEDGMENTS

Doubt, while important to a healthy faith, often emerges from suffering and may well lead to more. An acknowledgment, then, could go something like this: "I'm grateful to my friend who caused me more pain than I thought I could bear, but to my great surprise, the whole sorry ordeal made my faith stronger." And it would be true. But faith, I've learned, is larger than tales of survival and renewal. It's about learning to see, even in the dark. I've been blessed immeasurably to walk with people who have helped me see.

No one comes close to matching the influence of my parents, Leon and Iris. They were people of character. They were exceedingly wise. They had a reputation for integrity. They loved their family. They had great faith. There were hundreds of ordinary moments in my life in which their faith, not mine, opened my eyes to the inbreaking of God.

My brothers, Randy and Jim, not only shared with me our family story and many of the same relationships, but we have walked similar journeys of faith, which began with our parents. The church of our childhood was lifegiving and loving, but it was also legalistic at times. I rarely heard the grace of God taught there until I was well into high school. We three boys, however, heard about grace at home. From our father. All the time. Grace was the heart of things for him and, therefore, for us. No matter what you've done, he would tell us, in Christ you stand sinless before God. Not that you earned it—God's forgiveness is a free gift. Receive it, embrace it, then go and live graciously. Those lessons live with me still. And today, at least in part, it's because of our dad's words and commitments that not only we brothers, but also the church of our childhood, are grace-filled and mercy-driven. And it's why, even with the doubts, my own faith perseveres.

I'm awed by the kind of men my brothers are. To this day, when we get together, it's spiritual stuff we talk about. Not exclusively, of course. We talk about our families and work. And, the older we get, about our various ailments and the growing array of pharmaceutical interventions. But the overarching topic of our conversations is always the work of God in our lives—our church life, the books we are reading, the ministries we're involved in, the challenges we face, the hope we hold. We've shared a great deal over the years. I would not be the person I am were it not for Randy and Jim.

Beyond my childhood family, the list of names of those who in some way shaped my faith is larger than my brain's memory bank can hold. I will mention only a few who specifically impacted the writing of this book.

I grew up alongside an unusual group of boys, bound by a rare closeness that stretched from early childhood through college, years marked by growing maturity and deepening faith. And we had a lot of maturing to do, as exemplified by our possibly unwise line-dancing party late at night in a law office lobby. After college, we scattered to the winds and often go years without seeing one another. But if any of us faced a crisis today, none of us would hesitate to drop whatever we were doing to come help. Barry, Bobby, Danny, David, David, and Kent—I am grateful.

I suspect I've learned more about faith from my children—Jessica, Jocelyn, and Jay—than they've learned from me. When I see you, dear ones, and when I see your amazing spouses and your adorable, exceptionally bright children, I see Jesus. You've inspired much of what I've written and what I believe about God and about faith.

Ken and Mary Greene profoundly changed me—by their radical welcome, in gripping sermons and challenging conversations, in the "Well?" and the "Glory Hallelujah!" and over pancakes, laughter, and renewed hope. Don and Ellen Williams challenged me to do more than preach about poverty but to do something about it. Then they taught me how to do it by allowing me to walk beside them. Jim and Mignon Martin, dear friends for more than four decades, read early drafts of the book. They have been ceaselessly encouraging, not just in this project but in life. Jim has been not only my friend but also my physician. He helped me understand what was happening inside my body and offered both medical and spiritual advice.

Wilmose Kiplagat, my old student and dear friend, welcomed me into the depths of Christian community in Kenya years ago. More recently, he reconnected me with his fellow Kenyan David Busienei, whose story of sacrifice—selling his only cow, in essence giving up everything he had, to follow Jesus—has inspired me and countless others. I'm deeply grateful to them both. Dr. Samuel Twumasi-Ankrah, president of Heritage Christian University in Accra, Ghana, and his wife, Theresa, have taught me over the years the true meaning of *Akwaaba*, of Christian hospitality and intimate friendship. They are always welcome in my heart and in our home.

Anne Simpson and Daz Farrell, who are faith leaders in Australia, have become—along with Anne's husband, Dean, and Daz's wife, Ali—among Lesa's and my dearest life companions. Anne and Daz spent hours on video calls with us these last few months, engaging in dialogue about early chapters of the book, offering thoughtful critiques and encouragement, and giving me permission to share a slice of their own faith stories. Bob Randolph has been a spark of insight and energy in my adult life. His wisdom, accumulated through decades of ministry and his work with students and faculty as the chaplain to the institute at MIT, has been life-giving to me, especially in these last few months through regular phone conversations. He has taught me, as few others have, why good doubt is so important to faith.

David Sessions's sermons during the months I was writing intersected with my faith journey in surprising ways, sparking fresh imagination and new insights. Our conversations introduced me to valuable resources and brought clarity to my thinking. Doug Foster met with me almost every week, offering not only wise counsel, drawn from his expertise as a historian and church leader, but also spiritual nourishment and unwavering friendship. Luke Perkins met me frequently for coffee and conversation. He listens well, and his insights are both perceptive and grounding. John and Kim Hodges came to the house often, eating with us, singing with us, laughing with us, reflecting the kind of friendship that restores the soul. John read an early draft of the book with care and great discernment, offering suggestions that prompted me to take several chapters in new directions.

Eerdmans has been especially helpful in guiding the book to completion. It's an uncommon publishing company in the best of ways. The Eerdmans team holds extremely high standards but pairs them with a generous and compassionate spirit. They know what a good book looks like and push hard to make every book better. At the same time, they trust the author, and they listen. I'm especially grateful to Kimberley Benedict, who has been both encouraging and discerning, who recognized some holes in the narrative that I had missed, and who challenged me to rewrite some material that I loved but that wouldn't have benefited the readers as much as I thought. She was right. And the book is better for it. This is the second book for which Jenny Hoffman has served as my copyeditor. Her considerable editing skills, attention to tone and detail, professionalism, competence, and sheer kindness are rare. Whenever I see an email from Jenny or Kim pop into my inbox, I open it eagerly, knowing I'm in good hands.

One last word. I dedicated the book to my wife, MaLesa. She is more than worthy of such acknowledgment, as anyone who knows her will affirm. But she was also essential to the shaping of the book and to the spiritual journey behind it. She gave me courage when we didn't know whether my health would get better. She didn't hide her concerns, but she always seemed to live with a little more faith than I did, and so my own faith grew.

Lesa is also a scholar, a teacher, a thinker, a reader of books and people. Most evenings, for the last several months, I read to her what I had written that day. She listened. She encouraged. She let me know when my attempts at humor were funny and when they were, well, not so much. She shed tears with me and prayed with me. She provided perspective, a keen ear for words and metaphors, and often new directions for me to consider. This book—and my life—bear the imprint of her faith. I am blessed that each day the hope we share rises with the dawn, stirs our laughter, steadies our faith, and gives us just enough light to see the road that leads us home.

NOTES

Introduction

1. Christian Wiman, *My Bright Abyss: Meditation of a Modern Believer* (Farrar, Straus and Giroux, 2013), x.

2. James 1:6. Scripture citations are from the New Revised Standard Version Updated Edition (NRSVue) unless otherwise indicated.

3. Luke 6:37.

4. Luke 7:43.

5. Hebrews 5:14.

6. Hebrews 11:1.

Chapter 01

1. Mark 9:24.

2. Frederick Buechner, *Wishful Thinking: A Seeker's ABC*, rev. and expanded ed. (HarperOne, 1993), 24.

Chapter 02

1. Martin Marty, *A Cry of Absence: Reflections for the Winter of the Heart* (HarperCollins, 1983).

2. Marty, *Cry of Absence*, 4–5.

Chapter 03

1. Genesis 11:5.

2. Genesis 15:17.

3. Genesis 32:24–32; Hosea 12:4–5.

4. Judges 6:13 NIV.

5. 1 Samuel 3:21.

6. 1 Kings 3:5; 9:2; 11:9.

7. Richard Elliott Friedman, *The Hidden Face of God* (HarperOne, 1996), 16–17.
8. Numbers 12:6–8.
9. 1 Kings 18.
10. 1 Kings 19.
11. 1 Kings 19:10–12.
12. Genesis 19:22.
13. Psalm 8:5.
14. Deuteronomy 32:20.
15. Psalm 10:1.
16. Psalm 13:1.
17. Psalm 69:17.
18. Isaiah 54:7–8.
19. 1 Corinthians 13:12.
20. Psalm 22:29–31.

Chapter 04

1. John 14:16.
2. C. S. Lewis, *Surprised by Joy: The Shape of My Early Life* (Harcourt Brace, 1955), 166.
3. Lewis, *Surprised by Joy*, 168.
4. Lewis, *Surprised by Joy*, 191.
5. Lewis, *Surprised by Joy*, 78.
6. This 182-line poem can be found in multiple sources. It was first published in 1890 by the periodical *Merry England* 15, no. 87 (July 1890): 163–68.
7. Lewis, *Surprised by Joy*, 238.

Chapter 05

1. Evans E. Crawford, *The Hum: Call and Response in African American Preaching* (Abingdon, 1995), 13.
2. John Henry Newman, *An Essay on the Development of Christian Doctrine*, 6th ed. (University of Notre Dame Press, 1989, 2015), 40.
3. Barbara A. Holmes, *Joy Unspeakable: Contemplative Practices of the Black Church* (Fortress, 2017), 20.
4. Holmes, *Joy Unspeakable*, 20.
5. Holmes, *Joy Unspeakable*, 21.

Chapter 06

1. 1 Corinthians 1:10–17.
2. 1 Corinthians 1:22.
3. Mark 8:11–12.
4. Luke 21:5–7.
5. John 6:2.
6. John 4:48.
7. John 6:14.
8. John 6:15.
9. John 6:26.
10. John 6:26.

11. 1 Corinthians 14:1–25.
12. 1 Corinthians 14:26.
13. 1 Corinthians 12:31; 13:1–2.
14. John 20:25.
15. John 20:29.

Chapter 07

1. 1 Corinthians 8:1.
2. The most accessible and helpful discussion I know of concerning modern disenchantment and its implications for Christian faith comes from Richard Beck in his book *Hunting Magic Eels: Recovering an Enchanted Faith in a Skeptical Age* (Broadleaf, 2021). Also see Jason Ananda Josephson-Storm, *The Myth of Disenchantment: Magic, Modernity, and the Birth of the Human Sciences* (University of Chicago Press, 2017), who questions whether modern secularization and disenchantment are causally linked. Much of the current discussion can be traced to the work of contemporary Canadian philosopher Charles Taylor, *A Secular Age* (Belknap, 2007), and American sociologist Peter Berger, *The Sacred Canopy* (Anchor/Doubleday, 1967). Both drew insights from Max Weber.
3. Max Weber, "Science as a Vocation," in *From Max Weber: Essays in Sociology*, ed. and trans. Hans H. Gerth and C. Wright Mills (Oxford University Press, 1946), 155.
4. Romans 12:16.
5. Romans 11:25.
6. "Hurricane Katrina: Wrath of God? Religious Debate on Natural Disaster Comes to 'Scarborough Country,'" *NBC News*, October 5, 2005, https://www.nbcnews.com/id/wbna9600878.
7. Joe Brown, "Religious Conservatives Claim Katrina Was God's Omen, Punishment for the United States," *Media Matters for America*, September 13, 2005, https://www.mediamatters.org/hurricanes/religious-conservatives-claim-katrina-was-gods-omen-punishment-united-states.
8. Ecclesiastes 8:17.
9. D. Graham Burnett, "Will the Humanities Survive Artificial Intelligence?," *New Yorker*, April 26, 2025, https://www.newyorker.com/culture/the-weekend-essay/will-the-humanities-survive-artificial-intelligence.
10. Luke 24:13–35.
11. 2 Corinthians 11:6.

Chapter 08

1. Brandi Carlile, *Broken Horses: A Memoir* (Crown, 2021), 61–62.
2. Deuteronomy 11:18; "upon," "on," or "in" depending on the English translation.
3. Proverbs 3:3; 7:3.
4. Romans 10:10.
5. Deuteronomy 21:22–23.
6. 1 Corinthians 1:21–25.

Chapter 09

1. John 18:17.
2. Amos 5:21.
3. Isaiah 1:13, 15.
4. Isaiah 1:17.
5. Micah 6:8.
6. 1 Peter 5:12.
7. 1 Peter 1:6.
8. 1 Peter 2:12, 19–20; 3:9, 13.
9. 1 Peter 4:1–2.
10. 1 Peter 5:9–10.
11. E.g., 1 Peter 1:1; 2:11.
12. David French, "Why Are So Many Christians So Cruel?," *New York Times*, December 22, 2024.
13. E.g., Joe Rigney, *The Sin of Empathy: Compassion and Its Counterfeits* (Canon Press, 2025). Note David French's discussion of this phenomenon in his opinion piece, "Behold the Strange Spectacle of Christians Against Empathy," *New York Times*, February 13, 2025.

Chapter 10

1. "Turrentine Family History," http://www.old-new-orleans.com/Turrentine_History.html, "Black, White Turrentines Trace Heritage to N.C. Farm," *United Methodist News Service*, September 25, 2001, https://archive.wfn.org/2001/09/msg00274.html.
2. Edward Ball, *Slaves in the Family* (Ballantine Books, 1998), 416.
3. "Turrentine Family 2003," Turrentine Family Association, https://www.slideshare.net/slideshow/turrentine-family-presentation-2023/258166284; G. R. Turrentine, "Alexander Turrentine and His Descendants: A Case History of an Amateur Genealogist," *Arkansas Historical Quarterly* 10, no. 1 (Spring 1951): 58–66.
4. Carlile, *Broken Horses*, 82.
5. Carlile, *Broken Horses*, 149.
6. Carlile, *Broken Horses*, 86.
7. Luke 5:27–32.

8. Luke 6:9.

9. Luke 18:25.

10. Proverbs 16:5.

11. Proverbs 6:16–19.

12. Deuteronomy 25:13–16.

13. Luke 14:15–24.

Chapter 11

1. Originally *Maximes spirituelles* in French, there are dozens of translations of *The Practice of the Presence of God.* Any translation is worth spending some time with.

2. Matthew 5:45.

3. Luke 1:52–53.

4. Luke 6:20–21.

5. This concept was first described in an article by Paul F. Lazarsfeld and Robert K. Merton, "Mass Communication, Popular Taste and Organized Social Action," in *The Communication of Ideas*, ed. Lyman Bryson (University of Illinois Press, 1948; repr. in the Bobbs-Merrill Reprint Series in the Social Sciences [Bobbs-Merrill, 1957]).

6. Ronald Rolheiser, *The Holy Longing: The Search for Christian Spirituality* (Image Publishing, 1999), 98.